Preparing to Be President

The Memos of Richard E. Neustadt

Edited by Charles O. Jones

The AEI Press

Publisher for the American Enterprise Institute

WASHINGTON, D.C.

2000

Available in the United States from the AEI Press, c/o Publisher Resources Inc., 1224 Heil Quaker Blvd., P.O. Box 7001, La Vergne, TN 37086-7001. To order, call 1-800-269-6267. Distributed outside the United States by arrangement with Eurospan, 3 Henrietta Street, London WC2E 8LU, England.

Library of Congress Cataloging-in-Publication Data

Neustadt, Richard E.
Preparing to be president: the memos of Richard E. Neustadt / edited by Charles O. Jones.
p. cm.
Includes bibliographical references and index.
ISBN 0-8447-4139-6 (cloth: alk. paper)
1. Presidents—United States. 2. United States—Politics and government—1945–1989. 3. United States—Politics and government—1989– I. Jones, Charles O. II. Title.

JK516.N39 2000
352.23'0973'09045—dc21

00-058656

ISBN 0-8447-4139-6 (cloth: alk. paper)

1 3 5 7 9 10 8 6 4 2

The AEI Press
Publisher for the American Enterprise Institute
1150 17th Street, N.W.
Washington, D.C. 20036

Printed in the United States of America

Contents

Part 3
Neustadt Memos from Reagan to Clinton

Part 4
The Author's Reflections

Foreword

Richard E. Neustadt is the dean of presidential scholars. Beginning with *Presidential Power* in 1960, he reconceived the way Presidents, Washington elites, and the public understand the office of the Presidency. In particular, Neustadt showed all of us how Presidents can muster informal power to supplement their constitutional powers so as to govern effectively. He understood that a President could not rely on his title to get things done, but that he must use his persuasive powers to bring along Congress, the executive branch, his staff, his party, and the public.

While *Presidential Power* is known to every student of politics, it is less known that Neustadt devoted a great deal of energy to a particular aspect of presidential governance—how a new President makes a successful transition into office and begins to govern. In a series of largely private memos, Neustadt advised presidential candidates, Presidents-elect, and Presidents how to shape an administration to hit the ground running. In these memos, we see Neustadt's analysis at its best, always aware of the outlines of the presidential office, the other players in Washington, and the particular qualities of the President himself.

The memos are of great historical interest, but that is not their primary value. They are of lasting consequence and contemporary relevance because Neustadt puts his observations and insights into the context of the particular needs of a President and his times. Forty years ago, in his first memo to then-Senator John F. Kennedy, he began by distinguishing JFK's transition in 1960 from FDR's in 1932. Effective presidential governance requires attention to history, but also a realization that no timeless formula exists for a good transition or the success of a President.

We owe a debt of gratitude to Neustadt for agreeing to make these memos public and to write a new essay on the role of the transition adviser. His great concern that presidential transitions are critical times in American politics and that they do not always go as smoothly as they might was sufficient motivation. We are also deeply grateful to Charles O. Jones for selecting these memos from the corpus of Neustadt's work, editing the selections, and writing a very informative introduction. Jones's own seminal work on presidential transitions, *Passages to the Presidency: From Campaigning to Governing,* was published by the Brookings Institution Press in 1998. James Baker III, Paul Brountas, Robert B. Reich, Reed Hundt, and the late Diane Blair granted permission to publish the memos addressed to them. We are most grateful for their cooperation.

The timing of the publication of these memos could not be more appropriate. We will elect a new President in November, and on January 20, 2001, the reins of power will be transferred for the first time in eight years. The richly contextual view of presidential transitions taken by Neustadt and Jones is consistent with the spirit of the Transition to Governing Project, under whose auspices this book is being published. The project, which is generously funded by the Pew Charitable Trusts, aspires to improve the conditions for governing by shaping the way in which campaigns are waged and covered by the press and by encouraging early and thoughtful transition planning and implementation.

As codirectors of the Transition to Governing Project, we would like to offer special thanks to the Pew Charitable Trusts, whose president, Rebecca Rimel, has championed efforts to improve the quality of campaigning and governing. Paul Light, then director of public policy programs at Pew and now director of governmental studies at the Brookings Institution, was instrumental in conceiving and launching the project. Michael Delli Carpini, the current director of public policy programs at Pew, made a smooth midproject transition into office and offered tremendous support to our efforts. Elaine Casey, also with Pew, monitored our progress and shepherded us through day-to-day difficulties. In addition, Charles O. Jones acknowledges the support of the Glenn B. and Cleone Orr Hawkins Chair in Political Science, University of Wisconsin-Madison, and the John M. Olin Visiting Professorship in American Government, Nuffield College, Oxford University.

John Fortier, the project administrator, very effectively moved this volume to successful completion and has skillfully managed the larger effort of which it is a part. The presidents of our respective research organizations, Christopher DeMuth of the American Enterprise Institute and Michael Armacost of Brookings, provided crucial institutional support. Monty Brown, director of the AEI Press, steered the book through the editing and production process. Leigh Tripoli edited the manuscript.

The views expressed in this volume are those of the author and editor and should not be ascribed to the organizations listed above or to the trustees, officers, or other staff members of the American Enterprise Institute or the Brookings Institution.

Norman J. Ornstein
Resident Scholar
American Enterprise Institute

Thomas E. Mann
Senior Fellow
The Brookings Institution

Part 1

The Editor's Introduction

The Truman Aide Turned Professor

In his "later reflections" on the "hazards of transition," Richard E. Neustadt wrote:

> Everywhere there is a sense of a page turning, a new chapter in the country's history, a new chance too. And with it, irresistibly, there comes the sense, "they" couldn't, wouldn't, didn't, but "we" will. We just have done the hardest thing there is to do in politics. Governing has got to be a pleasure by comparison: We won, so we can! The psychology is partly that of having climbed one mountain so that the next looks easy, partly that of having had a run of luck that surely can't turn now![1]

Neustadt acknowledged the "arrogance" that is endemic to this experience, along with the attention and ceremony that feed and nurture it. Therein lies the challenge for Presidents-elect and their entourage to insinuate themselves into a working government when they often lack the experience and modesty to do so effectively.

Presidential candidate John F. Kennedy looked forward to the tasks of governing. He was engaged in one of the closest and most intense presidential elections in history—challenging a sitting Vice President to one of the most popular Presidents of all time. And yet he found the time and generated the interest during the campaign to ponder the transition to governing. It does all start there—with the candidate. For when the campaign ends, the answer to "What do we do now?" is quite simple: You govern. National and world attention is directed to the winner, who is expected to take charge. The recent candidate, now President-elect, is charged with creating a structure to be layered into the permanent government. The top is about to be lopped off every organizational unit, and the new leader has to replace and interlace. No one knows exactly how it should be done because each experience is necessarily unique to the people and the purposes to be served. Yet the new team is expected to display confidence in its capacity for control and to articulate its mission and priorities. This uniquely American exercise calls for the candidate to think ahead.

Substantial evidence exists that Kennedy engaged in forward thinking and encouraged it in others. Many years later, Neustadt offered these reflections on the postelection mood of the Kennedy team: "Part of the brilliance was that those people could not wait to start governing. They were so glad the campaign was over. Within three hours they were getting ready to do what they wanted to do. . . . [T]he season of governing was real for those people."[2] Neustadt had contributed to those preparations. Then a professor of government at Columbia University, he published a much acclaimed book, *Presidential Power,* in the spring of 1960 that displayed extraordinary understanding of the reach and limits of White House leadership. The book founded a political realism in presidential scholarship that would influence the study of leadership from that time forward.

Neustadt had served in the Truman administration and was, therefore, well acquainted with Clark Clifford, special counsel to Truman. Candidate Kennedy asked Clifford to think ahead to the transition. Kennedy reportedly said: "If I am elected, I don't want to wake up on the morning of November 9 and have to ask myself 'What in the world do I do now?'"[3] The Brookings Institution had created a study group on the presidential transition and urged both presidential candidates to prepare for the postelection period. Clifford began attending sessions of the Brookings Institution group as Kennedy's liaison person.[4] Clifford also lined up Neustadt, a junior associate from Truman's time, to give him some help with Kennedy's assignment.

By coincidence, the chairman of the Democratic National Committee, Senator Henry M. Jackson (D-Washington), had also asked Neustadt to prepare a memorandum on the transition. Jackson himself was interested in organizational and policy leadership issues. Among his other assignments, Jackson chaired the Senate Subcommittee on Organizational Issues in Defense and Diplomacy. The work of that subcommittee came to be directly useful to the Kennedy team in its consideration of national security structure and advice-giving. Neustadt completed his first memorandum, "Organizing the Transition," on September 15. Three days later, Senator Jackson arranged for Neustadt, memo in hand, to meet Kennedy at the candidate's Georgetown home. The rest of the story is told by Neustadt in Part 4. The story includes Kennedy's strictures against premature collaboration between Neustadt and Clifford. After the election was time enough to put their advice together, which Kennedy then did. Together, the two served as his nearest equivalent—not very near—to a modern "transition team."

Clifford and Neustadt were bound to provide different forms of advice, if not strikingly different recommendations. Clifford was the quintessential Washington insider. His usefulness was as much in who he was as in what he might say. He was a human switchboard. To know him was to have access to most others of importance for forming a Democratic White House. His memo was quite general in nature. It stressed the policy context, according to Arthur Schlesinger, and, interestingly, avoided any details—including names—that might prove embarrassing later. Thus, a reading today of Clifford's memo is of limited value. It is acknowledged historically as an important document, but Clifford's true value at the time was more for his contacts and personal counsel.

Neustadt's perspective was that of a different type of insider—less that of Washington, more that of governing. Please note my choice of *governing* rather than *government*. The "Washington" insider, like Clifford, is the contact person with power holders in, out of, and alongside government. The "government" insider may be a savvy bureaucrat, one who understands the nature and importance of structure, rules, administration, and organization. Many such may be found in the Office of Management and Budget. The "governing" insider concentrates on critical relationships between politics and administration. That sort of insider embraces the legitimacy of elective leaders to orchestrate the permanent government. As a governing insider, Neustadt specialized in fathoming presidential leadership. How could the President maximize effective use of status in a system of separated institutions sharing powers? That perspective provided a prism through which to treat the manifold issues of the transition. Central to Neustadt's analysis and advice-giving were these questions: How does the President view the job? How does he work best? What does he want to accomplish?

It is because of Neustadt's role and outlook as a governing insider that his memos to Kennedy merit publication forty years later. In those memos, Neustadt speaks to all presidential candidates and Presidents-elect. The central task is that of organizing a Presidency to achieve the goals and purposes of the incumbent. Neustadt has clear advice as to what constitutes effective organization to those ends. But he seldom, if ever, digresses from the core view that it is the President's mission that counts. Thus, he frequently advises that whatever he (Neustadt) suggests should be judged by the President's purpose, style, and perception of the job. Sometimes his view was more instructional—the professor to the student—than merely suggestive. Sometimes it simply confirmed what the President-elect might already believe. Here are examples from the second memo ("Staffing the President-Elect"): "Define in your own mind the staff jobs for which you feel a concrete, immediate need in the weeks ahead." "Do not let me or anyone else talk you into anything." "At this stage, I urge you to consider only needs of the first sort—your own." It was perhaps because of Kennedy's awareness of Neustadt's perceptiveness that he reportedly once observed that his adviser "makes everything a President does seem too premeditated."[5]

However contrasting their "insider" styles and skills, Clifford and Neustadt reinforced a central maxim: You, Mr. President-elect, must prepare yourself to shape your Presidency to suit your preferences. Arthur Schlesinger reported it this way: "The Clifford-Neustadt emphasis on molding the executive machinery to meet the needs of the President was exactly what Kennedy wanted."[6] Theodore Sorensen noted that the memos "in no way conflicted and largely coincided."[7] And Clark Clifford later wrote that "even if they [the memos] differed in details or emphasis, I knew that their overall thrust would be the same, urging measures to assure strong Presidential control of the executive branch."[8] Those results confirmed the sagacity of selecting the two types of insiders for advice and insisting that they work independently.

The Kennedy Memos

The Kennedy transition had many special characteristics. Kennedy succeeded one of the most popular Presidents in history, Dwight D. Eisenhower. Democrats had been out of the White House for eight years but had majorities in the House of Representatives and the Senate for the previous six years, the last two with a huge advantage in each chamber. Congressional Democrats were used to sharing in governing and might expect to continue to do so with a Democratic President. Two of those congressional Democrats—John F. Kennedy and Lyndon B. Johnson—were now to occupy the White House. Kennedy was unlikely to pattern his Presidency after that of a military commander. His political experience had been entirely in Congress—four years in the House of Representatives, eight years in the Senate. He did not rise to a leadership position in either chamber. Also relevant for his transition planning was the fact that his running mate did rise to leadership in the Senate. Lyndon Johnson served in the House for twelve years, where he was mentored by Speaker Sam Rayburn, and in the Senate for another twelve years, where he was majority leader for six years. Johnson's presence alone provided a strong stimulus for Kennedy to begin early in specifying his purposes and then molding the Presidency to meet *his* needs.

Also relevant, as reflected in the Neustadt memos, was the potential for cooperation from the Eisenhower team. Another pressure, deeply felt, stemmed from the unexpected narrowness of Kennedy's election, his plurality but .2 percent of the two-party popular vote. The general had not been a strongly partisan President. His organization stressed efficiency through a command structure. A legislative type like Kennedy was unlikely to emulate that structure. But he could benefit from its devotion to order and purpose over partisanship. Among other advantages, the Eisenhower manner had the effect of identifying public servants whom Kennedy might appoint as a display of bipartisanship. The Neustadt memos exhibit sensitivity to those conditions for forming a Kennedy administration, with frequent warnings about the effects of maintaining what is already there and encouragement to benefit from what will work well for the new President.

The first three memos offer a coherent set of guidelines for taking charge, all posited in the context of the President-elect's having decided what his Presidency is about. These three, "Organizing the Transition," "Staffing the President-Elect," and "Cabinet Departments: Some Things to Keep in Mind," provide topical advice, historical experience, attention to the Eisenhower operation, and reminders of what should continue and why. While comprehensive and instructive (though never tedious), the memos emphasize the choices that have to be made. Neustadt never forgets who it is that will be the President.

In the first memo (September 15, 1960), Neustadt provided a review of basic issues associated with the transition—the pressures of meeting expectations in the first 100 days; deciding what the message will be; selecting the most trusted aides—in the White House and within the executive; designating the cabinet; organizing the process for subcabinet appointments; initiating liaison to and reassuring the bureaucracy, Congress, the outgoing administration, and the press; arranging to move into the White House and the government; and preparing for the first cabinet meetings and the inaugural. It truly is a memo for all time, ever sensitive to who the President is and what he wants to do, as well as citing caveats regarding preinaugural traps: "The period before Inauguration Day is . . . a time for caution." "Appoint men only to jobs for which the President-elect, himself, feels an immediate and continuing need, a need he has defined in his own mind, and can at once define for them." Small wonder Senator Kennedy wanted more after reading this first briefing paper.

The second memo (October 30, 1960) directs attention to staffing needs. In the opening paragraphs, Neustadt stresses the singularity of a President's needs. He repeated points made in the first memo: "A President's needs for staff are bound to be different in many ways from a senator's, or even from a candidate's. But your needs in the Presidency will also differ from Eisenhower's." He then defined the challenge for the President-elect in fashioning his staff: Clarify your needs first. "You are the only person you can count on to be thinking about what helps you." Then, consider the needs others have for presidential help.

Notable in this second missive is attention to the experience of other Presidents. Sensing that Kennedy's own preference was for the more collegial staff of Franklin Delano Roosevelt, Neustadt explained the responsibilities of that style: "A collegial staff has to be managed; competition has to be audited. To run a staff in Roosevelt's style imposes heavy burdens." As reinforcement, Neustadt attached summaries of Roosevelt's approaches to staffing the White House and the Bureau of the Budget. The first of those summaries remains one of the most succinct and sophisticated treatments of the Roosevelt style of governing ever written. It was, understandably, welcomed by Kennedy for the lessons it contained.

In the text of the second memo, Neustadt provided detailed analysis and comments on specific staff positions, including the timing of appointments and the liaison required for various positions. The relevance for now is less in those details than in the historical context Neustadt creates as well as the identification of the range of assignments and connections for all Presidents-elect. Also pertinent is the identification of consequences for taking one course or another, again with historical references.

The third memo in this collection (November 3, 1960) is directed to cabinet departments. Neustadt clarifies that his purpose is not to be involved in various political criteria for appointments. Rather, consistent with his overarching theme, Neustadt identifies factors "worth your while to keep in mind." "These bear upon your own ability as President to conserve your freedom of action and to guard your reputation." Once again we have an orientation that justifies publishing these memos today, that is, an understanding of the effects of making appointments of persons who then act for the President in their governing capacities. The discussion of the Department of the Treasury is especially insightful. Notable is Neustadt's advice to a Democratic President to consider a Republican for the post, an action later taken by Kennedy with the appointment of Douglas Dillon. Also highlighted is the Department of Justice, where "the full utility . . . as a presidential asset has not often been perceived by sitting Presidents." Failure to be so attentive can cause (and has caused) Justice to be "a passive drag or a decided liability." Not all departments were included as not presenting special problems for the President's status.[9]

Two other memos, the seventh (December 20, 1960) and twelfth (January 26, 1961) in this collection, also deal with cabinet matters. The seventh warned Kennedy about designating "cabinet assistants" because expectations may then quickly develop that Eisenhower's cabinet system would be adopted.

Neustadt counsels against immediate acceptance of procedures in place as cabinet secretaries orient themselves to their new jobs. He points out that "vested interests in the present cabinet system would spring up in each of your departments." His advice to Kennedy can be summarized this way: Do not let the past determine your future.

The twelfth memo he prepared with Fred Dutton. In offering remarks for the first cabinet meeting, Neustadt and Dutton supply a concept of cabinet use. They stressed "proposals for action" over "what is wrong," "personal and public loyalty," presidential control of the agenda, and limiting attendance. "Let us not waste time" was essentially advice to make cabinet meetings purposeful and to avoid a routine of meetings for their own sake. That advice was, no doubt, welcomed by a President who did not favor meetings and undervalued Ike's use of cabinet meetings to bind members to him personally, by playing on their sense of reflected glory.

The fourth (December 3, 1960) and fifth (December 7, 1960) memos in this collection are brief and yet are among the most revealing of the subtleties of Neustadt's understanding of the White House and his client. Consistent with the collegial style of White House organization, the advice was for Kennedy to be cautious in designating titles for staff. Titles should be "unspecific" so as to permit shifting assignments and to prevent "automatic formation of a clientele with which the man is openly identified." That rationale led Neustadt to object to creating a specific assignment for representing "Negro" groups in the White House. He explained that such an appointment "would stick out like a sore thumb" in a White House staff with "five or six general-utility trouble shooters." He did not object to having such a liaison person, only to placing him on the White House staff. He pointed out, however, that "Senator Kennedy is not bound by any conceptions of mine."[10] No such person was appointed.

One other memo also treats staff issues. The eighth memo (December 23, 1960) in this collection returned to the matter of staff titles. Once again, Neustadt warned Kennedy to avoid a move that would invite emulation of Eisenhower's cabinet system. At issue was a title for Fred Dutton. Kennedy had mentioned "secretary of the cabinet." Neustadt forcefully stated that he "wouldn't touch this title with a ten-foot pole." As with his earlier memo on cabinet assistants, the argument was one of avoiding conclusions within the bureaucracy and the rest of the government "that you, like Ike, intend to try to use the cabinet, per se, as a major forum for policy-making." Here, as elsewhere, Neustadt promoted thinking about how Kennedy's organizational decisions would be read elsewhere—very much the perspective dominating his book on presidential power. Throughout, he argued that any signals sent should be evaluated for their consistency with Kennedy's real aims.

Three memos in this collection direct attention to the organization of specific functions: national security, disarmament, and science advising. The sixth memo (December 8, 1960) deals with one of the most sensitive issues within the executive—the role of the National Security Council staff to the Departments of State and Defense. As it happened, Senator Jackson's Subcommittee on Organizational Issues in Defense and Diplomacy had just completed its staff report on the NSC.

Neustadt had worked on that report. His brief sought to advise Kennedy about national security organizational and staffing issues that would arise before his inauguration—issues that would inevitably have effects later on. Its relevance today is precisely as an example of how actions taken in the transition period can either enhance or impede the President's flexibility once in office.

The ninth memo (January 2, 1961) deals with the location of the Disarmament Agency. Why include it? Simply because the organizational issue is generic—that of situating a cross-cutting function. Neustadt thinks through the implications and effects of a decision, blended, as always, with the clarity of the President's purposes. The tenth memo (January 4, 1961) considers the President's science adviser. It is illustrative of the special liaison required to communities that are vital to the work of government. It was a subject that Neustadt, an academic himself, was well qualified to handle. The challenge, as with other such contacts, was to maintain control and avoid the hardening of expectations by the community in question.

As with the first three, the eleventh memo (January 18, 1961) is a set of recommendations for all time. One feature is universal for new Presidents: they have never served in that position before (though some, Vice Presidents who become Presidents, sat close by). Associated is the understanding, as drawn from historical experience, that no one can quite know what it is like to be President in advance of serving. And so this memo directs attention to those early weeks when the President is taking a crash course on his job and during which time "flaps" are inevitable. Neustadt identifies the types of likely emergencies and how they will present themselves, along with advice on the "how and who" for handling them. Clearly evident in this memo are the complications of a President suddenly responsible for an emerging administration, with dozens of appointees, themselves learning their jobs, acting in his name. It should be pointed out that however wise Neustadt's counsel on the subject, it did not prevent the "Bay of Pigs" flap from occurring early in the Kennedy administration.[11]

Historical Lessons for James Baker III

The circumstances of Ronald Reagan's victory in 1980 were very different from those of Kennedy's win in 1960. Reagan defeated an incumbent President by a landslide in the Electoral College—the first defeat for an elected incumbent since Roosevelt crushed Hoover in 1932.[12] The campaign was strongly issue-oriented, with Reagan a devoted conservative promising to act decisively to reduce the government and improve the economy. Reagan's win was punctuated by Republicans' gaining a majority in the Senate for the first time since 1954 and increasing their numbers in the House of Representatives by thirty-four seats, the greatest increase for the party in a presidential election since 1920. The expectation was for strong leadership and significant policy change.

After Ronald Reagan's impressive win in 1980, Neustadt, then at Harvard University's Kennedy School of Government, was asked by his colleague, Jonathan Moore, to write a memo for James Baker III, Reagan's probable chief of staff. Moore, who had served in a number of posts in the Nixon administration, was director of the Institute of Politics at the Kennedy School. What Neustadt prepared was of a very different order from the memos written for Kennedy. Neustadt was part of the team in 1960, the governing insider. In 1980 he was the contemplative outsider. In that role, he provided a masterful review of the problems of staffing the White House. Predictably, he began with advice to build structure suited to "the man's preferred way of doing work." There it was again: Know the President; understand his style; make him effective in that context.

Following that orientation, Neustadt provided advice regarding mismatches in the operating styles of staff, the effects of how it was done last time, change for the sake of change, cabinet management and use, the association of foreign and domestic perspectives, and the prevention of staff growth (possibly producing "high-level loose cannons," as in Watergate). The lessons are richly illustrated with historical examples of the successes and failures of White House staff operations. Neustadt's reflections on the contrasting personal styles of Dean Rusk and Robert McNamara are particularly revealing. And, of course, the point is not to provide engrossing gossip about a past administration (no "kiss and tell" here). It is rather to encourage thought about how best to promote good advice for the President.

It is uncertain the extent to which Baker absorbed those specific lessons of history. No mention is made of Neustadt's memo in the various volumes on the organization of the Reagan Presidency.[13] Yet Neustadt's central maxim was clearly followed: Organize the White House staff to suit the needs and style of the incumbent. Reagan and Kennedy were both highly staff-dependent Presidents, though for different reasons: Reagan for having set goals, then delegating; Kennedy for having extended his reach with generalists like himself. Their transitions into office were among the more successful in recent decades.

Transition Planning Advice for Dukakis

Neustadt also advised presidential candidates who lost. His memo to Paul Brountas, a Michael Dukakis aide, is included here primarily because it treats the important matter of transition planning during the campaign. It is worth noting that the memo was written in late May 1988 when Dukakis was definitely competitive with George H. W. Bush in the polls. As indicated in the memo, Neustadt advised that those engaged in transition planning be integrated into the campaign, not "sitting on the sidelines as a postelection planner." He provided historical examples, noting the success of James Baker because he was a part of the 1980 Reagan campaign, not in the least a sideliner. Neustadt also portrayed the tensions between those working in the campaign and those planning for governing after. Those stresses are certain to occur; they are amplified if the planners are set off from the campaigners, as with the Carter and Clinton planning efforts.[14]

This memo also contains important advice regarding the differences between Washington and state capitals. Massachusetts is a state just larger than Georgia. Carter was the other Democratic governor to win the White House in the postwar period (before 1988). Therefore, Neustadt's sage advice was not to mistake a presidential transition for one in Boston or Atlanta. That observation then led him to offer rules of thumb, mostly derived from his experience in participating in and observing other transitions. The reader will detect yet again some familiar Neustadt canons: Know what it is you want to accomplish. Do not make change for its own sake. Do not accept what is there if it does not suit your purposes. Take help from those who are leaving if they are willing to give it.

The Clinton Memos

The Kennedy, Carter, and Clinton victories had characteristics in common. Their popular vote percentage was relatively low (Kennedy 49.7 percent, Carter 50.1 percent, Clinton 43.3 percent in a three-candidate race); the Kennedy and Carter Electoral College wins were modest, Clinton's somewhat more robust; Democrats had little or no gain in Congress (and a net loss of nine House seats in 1992). Differences also existed. Whereas Kennedy had fourteen years of experience in Congress and was part of an elite political family, Carter and Clinton were very much "out-of-towners." Their experience was that of southern governors of medium- and small-populated states with Democratic state legislatures. The effects of those conditions were similar, if somewhat differentially applicable. Each of those Presidents-elect had to compensate for the limitations of his political circumstances. The transition in each case was crucial for a positive beginning. For Clinton, the postelection period was especially sensitive, given the high expectations for the return of one-party government. As one analyst viewed it, "The stars are really aligned right for the next four years."[15]

By the time of Clinton's win, Neustadt had seen seven

Presidents come and go since the writing of his original memos. Still, his former student, Senator Albert Gore, Jr. (D-Tennessee), was on the ticket with Clinton, and one of his colleagues at Harvard, Robert B. Reich, was a close Clinton friend and the future secretary of labor. It was in response to Reich that Neustadt propounded ten "lessons" for the prospective transition. They were forwarded during August of 1992. One is struck by the greater urgency in making appointments recommended by Neustadt (compared with his advice to Kennedy). Also apparent is the greater sensitivity to institutional developments that made it even more imperative that an "out-of-towner" organize carefully. The clear implication of Neustadt's "lessons" was that the press, Congress, the bureaucracy, and the presidential branch[16] had all become significantly more active during the transition period and thereby increased the challenges for the new President. Finally, Neustadt advises Clinton not to repeat several of the mistakes of Jimmy Carter. Given the similarities in their political circumstances and experiences as southern governors, such guidance was appropriate. As it happened, however, much of Neustadt's counsel was ignored, and mistakes of the past were, in fact, repeated. Readers can, themselves, use the "lessons" as a checklist for rating the Clinton transition, which was uniformly criticized by political analysts, as well as by many Clinton staff and, later, by the President himself.[17] Somehow, the sensible counsel of that document got lost, as did the sound advice of other experienced transition aides with more direct access to the President and his entourage.

The other memos in this set are unique as transition documents. The first to Reed Hundt, a lawyer friend of Al Gore, addresses the case of the Vice President (specifically Neustadt's former student). In it, Neustadt identifies the "special vantage point" of the Vice President as the President's campaign and election partner. Therefore, if the President has the wit to acknowledge that advantage, he will have a second mind through which to pass the issues of the day. That mind will have been tempered too by the special political experience of running for the Presidency. No one else can perform that role, and therefore the Vice President needs to nurture it, starting with a familiar Boy Scout code, "Be prepared." Attached to the memo is a set of rules that are engaging, realistic, and relevant and that reveal the nature and purpose of the Vice Presidency.

The last memos in this set, and in this collection, direct attention to the role of the first lady. Here is a subject not usually considered as a transition issue apart from the personal adjustments made within the family. The case of Hillary Rodham Clinton was, however, very special. Voters were promised "two for the price of one." The future first lady had been actively involved in policy issues during her husband's service as governor of Arkansas, both within the state and nationally as president of the Children's Defense Fund. Most analysts believed that Mrs. Clinton would play a direct role in the new administration.

Neustadt's memo was a follow-up to a conversation he had with Professor Diane Blair, University of Arkansas-Fayetteville, at a postelection conference of campaign managers at Harvard University. The late Professor Blair was a close, personal friend of Mrs. Clinton. The topic was a White House title for the first lady. As with his other memos on titles, Neustadt explores the implications for the President of various alternatives. This point is critical and wholly consistent with Neustadt's orientation. He never loses focus. Even when it comes to the President's wife, the test is that of the effect on the Presidency. As always, Neustadt reviews historical cases as context for understanding Mrs. Clinton's position. Soon, he has detached her from a strictly personal role as wife to outline her political and institutional role as counselor and specifies the demands of that position and potential political effects.

Finally, Neustadt turns to the not-so-simple matter of the law. Regarding the employment of relatives, the *United States Code* reads: "A public official may not appoint, employ, promote, advance, or advocate for appointment, employment, promotion, or advancement, in or to a civilian position in the agency in which he is serving or over which he exercises jurisdiction or control any individual who is a relative of the public official."[18] It was Neustadt's judgment that even if ambiguities could be identified in that language, as with a possible distinction between "designation" and "appointment," problems would develop. As punctuation to that view, Neustadt forwarded a second memo to Professor Blair. In it he expressed the opinions of his wife, Shirley Williams, an experienced British politician. Her advice was direct and relevant. In the end, Mrs. Clinton was not given a formal title within the White House but was designated to chair the President's Task Force on National Health Reform, a post that also drew vigorous criticism.

It is altogether fitting that this collection of memos culminates with the advice of Neustadt and his wife on the role of the first lady. These memos illustrate virtually every feature of Neustadt's orientation toward and command of the Presidency. He never wavers from the perspective of fitting a President into the institution, sensitive always to the adjustments necessary for benefiting from what is new in the context of what is there. It is precisely that continuity in perspective that ensures the pertinence of these memos in 2000 and for future transitions.

Other Memos

Neustadt prepared other memos judged by the editor to be less immediately relevant. Several were specific to detailed matters of note at the time and have little or no bearing on current issues. Some treated relationships of the President to programs or agencies, for example, the Council of Economic Advisers, space programs and the National Aeronautics and Space Council, and the United States Information Agency. The Reorganization Act of 1949, as amended, had expired and thus encouraged renewal for the new Democratic President who planned organizational changes. That topic was the subject of a number of memos. Still other memos treated various personnel matters (including appointments), provided checklists of organizational issues to be cared for by the new team, and suggested language for press releases.

The Timelessness of Neustadt's Advice

The range and scope of these memos attest to the extraordinary knowledge and political savvy of this professor of politics. Few other scholars have so successfully bridged the divide between the academy and government. It is often said that much of the work on transitions is seen but not read. Not so with the advice of Dick Neustadt. As is evident from these memos, he has not pressed his counsel on others. Rather, he replies responsibly to requests from those close to Presidents-elect. The purpose of this book is to ensure that the timeless part of his advice becomes available for planning and effecting transitions in the future. Integral to that purpose is his advice to future advisers in which he reflects on his own experience and that of the Presidents he served. Those reflections he has written for this book, as a very special memo to its readers, who will find it in Part 4 as "Neustadt's Advises the Advisers in 2000." Presidency scholars too have legacies, none weightier than Dick Neustadt's, the Truman aide turned professor.

Part 2

Neustadt Memos for the Kennedy Transition

Memo 1
Organizing the Transition

For: Senator John F. Kennedy
(through Senator Henry M. Jackson, D-Washington)
September 15, 1960

1. The Problem of Another "Hundred Days"

One hears talk all over town about another "Hundred Days" once [Senator] Kennedy is in the White House. If this means an impression to be made on Congressmen, bureaucrats, press, public, foreign governments, the analogy is apt. Nothing would help the new administration more than such a first impression of energy, direction, action, *and* accomplishment. Creating that impression and sustaining it become prime objectives for the months after Inauguration Day. Since an impression of the [Franklin D.] Roosevelt's sort feeds on reality, and could not be sustained by mere "public relations," establishing conditions that will foster real accomplishment becomes a prime objective for the brief transition period before Inauguration Day.

But the "Hundred Days" analogy can also be taken—and is being taken—as an expectation of fulfillment for every sort of legislative promise in the platform and the campaign. Everybody tends to think of his pet pledge as the priority accomplishment for Kennedy's first three months. Yet that timing only brings us to the Easter Recess of the First Session of a modern Congress!

These legislative wants are hard to square with a convincing demonstration of energy and accomplishment. "Another

'Hundred Days'" as an impression of effectiveness is threatened by the promissory notes read into that analogy.

In terms of legislative action, the analogy to 1933 is not apt. Roosevelt then did not take office until March. He had four months to organize the takeover. Congress was adjourned when he entered the White House and was not due to assemble until December. It met in special session after his inauguration, on his call. It met, moreover, to deal with a devastating domestic crisis that was seen and felt by citizens, in their own lives, all across the country. Foreign relations, meanwhile, raised virtually no issues that could not be ignored or postponed. And Roosevelt had the patronage (old style) to dole out at a time when jobs of any sort were highly valued. What is the analogy with 1961?

In 1948, when [Harry S.] Truman was reelected, there also was much talk of "another 'Hundred Days.'" But when he was sworn in a second time, Congress had been in session for three weeks, organized, bills introduced, committees working. No sharply felt, widely perceived crisis faced the country. Instead, in all the realms of cold war and of welfare undertakings—most of them unknown in 1933—government agencies and private groups pressed diverse legislative claims, citing campaign promises as their authority and jostling each other in the rush to take advantage of Truman's "honeymoon." Weeks before the inaugural, the groups concerned had gained commitments from congressional leaders (whether they committed Truman, or he, them, is in dispute) for early floor fights on FEPC [Fair Employment Practices Committee] and on repeal of [the] Taft-Hartley [Act of 1947]. By the time those fights had failed, the "honeymoon" was over and the session far advanced with little else done. In legislative terms, it is 1949, not 1933, that offers an analogy and warnings—for 1961.

Unlike Truman, Kennedy may come into office in the midst of some sharp, overt international emergency, or in the train of a sharp economic slump. It is at least as possible, however, that January 1961 will be a time of many incipient crises but no "crisis." So was 1949.

It follows that, for the transition period between election and inaugural, the guidelines ought to be: *Postpone whatever is postponable* in the mechanics of administration building. Put off the novelties that have not been thought through. *Concentrate upon the things that are immediately relevant to showing real effectiveness* on and after January 20. And in the doing of those things, keep this objective uppermost. It is the key objective for the weeks after November 8 [Election Day].

The things that cannot be postponed are enumerated below. They are roughly in the order in which it seems desirable to deal with them, starting November 9.

2. Organizing for a First Message to Congress

The most important task in the transition is the working out of strategy and tactics for an exploitation of the "honeymoon" ahead. This means decisions on the substance, timing, publicity, and priority of legislative proposals to Congress. It means decisions of the same sort on discretionary executive actions. It means decisions on relationships between projected proposals and actions. It means weighing short-range gains against long-range troubles, political and other. It means judging what should be done in the President's name, and what should not, and how to enforce the distinction. It also means evaluating fiscal implications of proposals and of actions, both, and making some immediate decisions on taxation and the budget.

Not all of these decisions can be taken before January 20, but preparatory work needs to be far advanced by then: The issues should have been identified, the arguments defined, preliminary judgments entered well before Inauguration Day.

The way to get this work done is to organize its doing around presidential action by a certain date. The way to gain an action and to set a deadline is to make plans for an early message to Congress. The [Senator Henry M.] Jackson Subcommittee [on National Policy Machinery] has suggested a "Resources and Requirements Report," with foreign as well as domestic dimensions, to supplement the present annual messages on a regular basis. Without commitment at this time to regularity, the idea might be taken as a starting point in planning the new President's first message.

The first thing to do is to make a plan, deciding tentatively on the timing and the scope of such a message. This provides a target for everybody who has ideas, views, concerns about the program objectives of the new regime.

The second thing to do is to establish "working groups" and get them moving with the message as their target—both on things that should be asked of Congress and on things that could be pronounced done or underway administratively. . . . Prominent persons whose views have been solicited can be drawn into groups or treated as competitors and dealt with individually.

The third thing to do is to get a "bird-dog" on the scene, putting somebody in charge of staff work on the message. This should be someone close to Kennedy, very much in his confidence and very much a "staff man" (but a tough-minded one). His job should be to see that all the working groups are working, the competitors competing, gaps filled, issues raised, arguments brought to focus, and the President-elect informed on who is doing what, with what, to whom. This is a full-time job, for the whole transition period and after. Its holder has to be much more than a draftsman; drafting is merely his hunting license; his hunting ground is foreign and domestic program, legislative *and* administrative. This is somewhat like [Samuel] Rosenman's work at message season in the Roosevelt White House or like [Clark] Clifford's and [Charles] Murphy's in the Truman White House. But in many ways, it is a broader and rougher job than theirs; they worked in an established context; this man will not.

3. Designating White House Aides

After Election Day the President-elect will need a small personal staff to operate through the transition period and to take office with him. A few staff aides are immediately necessary; their names and jobs should be announced at once, so that importunate office seekers, idea peddlers, pressmen, legislators, diplomats, and cabinet designees know who and what they are. These necessary jobs include:

(a) A press secretary, whose work after inaugural will be so much like his work before that he should have the title at the outset. On November 9, Kennedy will be transformed in the eyes of Americans and foreign governments. He will no longer have the leeway of a "campaigner." His statements will be taken with the utmost seriousness. Everything said and done in public need be weighed as though he were already President.

(b) An appointments aide to guard the door and manage the daily schedule. Whether this person should be designated "appointments secretary" depends on whether he is meant to have autonomy, after inaugural, or to work as a subordinate of some other aide. If subordination is intended, hold off on the "secretary" part of that title.

(c) A "number-one boy," serving as a sort of first assistant on general operations, day by day. He could be called "executive assistant to the President-elect," and he could carry that title into the White House in lieu of Sherman Adams's title [in the Eisenhower Presidency], "*The* assistant to the President." It would be well to avoid reminders of Adams, not only for public relations but because, once in the White House, Kennedy may find that he needs several "number-one boys" for different aspects of the work; other things aside, Adams was a terrible bottleneck.

(d) The message-and-program aide indicated above. If the man is a lawyer, and if Kennedy wants him around for comparable work in later months, he might be designated "special counsel" (FDR's invention for Rosenman). But he could just as well be called "special consultant" and his long-run status left in abeyance for the time being. What counts in the short run is his standing with the President-elect, not his title.

(e) A personnel consultant (discussed below). Here, again, it would be well to treat the job as ad hoc and avoid traditional White House titles for the time being.

(f) A personal secretary who might remain just that after January 20, or who might carry higher status and more general duties afterwards, depending on the President's convenience and her capabilities. Meanwhile, it would be well not to dispose of any of the traditional titles one might ultimately want for her.

These six should suffice as a nucleus to move into the White House, January 20, where they will find the executive clerk and his career assistants on the job for routine paper processing. Additional aides will certainly be needed for ad hoc troubleshooting before inaugural; still more so afterwards. But until the needs are felt to be both clear and continuing, and until the men have been tried on the job, there is no reason to announce their designation as permanent members of the White House staff. Nor is there reason to give them traditional White House titles.

A President's needs for personal staff, and the relations among staff, are bound to be different in many ways from a senator's, or even from a presidential candidate's. But this President's needs and staff relations will also differ from Eisenhower's. Many of the needs and many of the differences cannot be fully understood, or met, until they have been experienced. They cannot be experienced until after January 20. The period before Inauguration Day is thus a time for caution.

In designating personal staff, two rules of thumb are indicated:

First, appoint men only to jobs for which the President-elect, himself, feels an immediate and continuing need, a need he has defined in his own mind, and can at once define for them. If the need is immediate but not continuing, offer a "consultantship," or put the man in a department and borrow him back.

Second, give appointees titles that square with the jobs to be done and choose no titles without thinking of their bureaucratic connotations in the outgoing regime. A title may attract a lot of "customary" business that the President-elect wants handled somewhere else, or not at all, or on which he prefers experimentation. A title also may connote a ranking in the staff that he does not intend.

If these rules of thumb are followed, most of Eisenhower's current staff positions will fall into abeyance on January 20. There is nothing wrong with that.

4. Designating Science and Security Aides

Two of the positions in Eisenhower's White House present special problems.

(a) The Science Adviser. This post, created after Sputnik, is highly valued in the scientific community, which would be disturbed if it were not filled by early December. But before it is filled, a special effort should be made to think through the sort of work for which a man is wanted, and hence the sort of man. Thought will expose some hidden difficulties.

(b) The Special Assistant for National Security Affairs. There will be no outside pressure for filling this post, and NSC [National Security Council] can operate without it for a time at least (see #17 below ["Arranging Initial Cabinet and NSC Meetings"]). But if, for reasons of his own, the President-elect wants to make an appointment, both the title and the duties should be considered, in advance, with particular regard for the intended role of the secretary of state, vis-à-vis NSC.

5. Designating Executive Office Aides

Soon after November 8, the President-elect will have use for a principal assistant, at one remove from personal aides, who can backstop the White House in coping with programming and administrative problems from Inauguration Day on. If he is to be of maximum assistance from the start, the job to give him is the budget directorship. With an early designation as budget director, he could be very useful *before* January 20, moving in tandem with the message aide and the working groups suggested above, to keep track of issues that cannot be settled by [inaugural] message time, or considered in message terms. (He could also be a temporary hitching post for miscellaneous career staffs in second-level jobs now housed inside the White House, which ought to be moved out of there and examined at leisure.)

This budget director–designate should be conceived as someone capable of broad-gauged, general-purposed service to the President, picking up the staff work that personal aides cannot give time to on a continuing basis. . . .

This person need not be the budget liaison man before inauguration (see #11 below ["Establishing Liaison with the Eisenhower Administration"]). Sitting in on Eisenhower's budget-making is the job for a reliable assistant with high capability as a reporter.

Besides the budget director, there are three top appointive officials in the Executive Office: The chairman of the Council of Economic Advisers [CEA], the director of the Office of Civilian Defense Mobilization [OCDM], and the executive secretary of NSC. With respect to these:

(a) The chairmanship of CEA need not be filled in a hurry. Undoubtedly, there needs to be an ad hoc working group . . . as part of the program preparation sketched in item #2 above ["Organizing for a First Message to Congress"]. But with this established and working, one can take time to decide what use one wants to make of CEA and how it is to fit with other staff machinery, before designating its chairman. These organizational decisions should come first because they have a bearing on what sort of man is wanted in the job. . . . Which kind of service is wanted?

(b) The directorship of OCDM should be left vacant and filled, after January 20, by the senior careerist on an "acting" basis. OCDM now combines mutually incompatible, poorly performed functions. What should be done with these functions needs a lot of thought and exploration. The end result might be abolition of OCDM. Meanwhile, caution counsels no director.

(c) The executive secretaryship of NSC has been filled since 1949 by James Lay, who acts as a careerist, neutral "secretary." There is no reason why he should not be kept on at least until Kennedy gets familiar with and decides what he wants to do with NSC and its subordinate machinery. Before inaugural, however, and immediately thereafter, Lay will need an ad hoc contact point with the incoming administration. . . .

6. Designating Cabinet Officers

There is no operating reason why cabinet officers and heads of major agencies need be designated immediately after election. With "working groups" established and key staff aides appointed (as suggested in items 2–5 above ["Organizing for a First Message to Congress," "Designating White House Aides," "Designating Science and Security Aides," and "Designating Executive Office Aides"]) one does not need cabinet officers in order to get moving toward a fast start after January 20. Indeed, there is advantage in holding off on most cabinet appointments until staff and working groups are launched; cabinet members then would have a framework to fit into and could not wander off on their own. As a rule of thumb: defer cabinet and major agency designations until early December.

A possible exception is the secretaryship of state. The Jackson Subcommittee [on National Policy Machinery] favors using the secretary not just as a department head but as a principal assistant in the whole sphere of national security policy. If the President-elect intends to take this line, the secretary should be the first cabinet member appointed. . . . On the other hand, some of the persons now competing for the secretaryship might not want that role, or could not sustain it. This also argues for early announcement, so that alternatives could be arranged promptly. Still another reason for early announcement is the competition. After election, it may be hard for working groups to work effectively in the national security sphere while the job is still open.

A second possible exception is the cabinet post, if any, where the present incumbent [in the Eisenhower administration] would be retained as a gesture of bipartisanship. Nothing of the sort may be contemplated. But if it is, then obviously the sooner it were done the better.

With these exceptions, cabinet designations could be left until early December. But they should not come much later. This leaves only about five weeks (including Christmas) for the men to wind up present obligations, get briefed on new ones, and contribute (if they can) to program preparation. In the interest of a fast start, briefing is the main thing. Working groups and presidential aides can carry program preparation before January 20; cabinet designees should concentrate on learning all they can about the workings, staffs, and budgets of their agencies. Five weeks is little enough time for that.

In choosing cabinet officers (and heads of major agencies), the President-elect will naturally consider the usual criteria of geographic, party, and interest-group "representativeness." Three additional criteria are worth bearing in mind:

First is competitive balance among major differences in policy outlook, on which Kennedy does not choose to make up his mind for all time. This is a very tricky and important problem in "representativeness." If the President-elect wants both "conservative" and "liberal" advice on economic management, for example, and wants the competition to come out where he can see it and judge it, he needs to choose strong-minded competitors, and he needs to put them in positions of roughly equal institutional power, so that neither wins the contest at a bureaucratic level too far down for the President to judge it. For example, if the Treasury (a powerful post) were given to a "conservative," it would not suffice to put his competition on the presidential staff; at least two cabinet competitors would be needed in addition.

Second is the chance for useful reorientation of a department's role with a change in its secretary's traditional orientation. The Eisenhower administration, for example, has had an industrial relations specialist as secretary of labor [James Mitchell], instead of the traditional union president or politician avowedly representing "labor's voice in the cabinet." As a result, [Secretary] Mitchell has been able to act for the administration in labor disputes and to keep a supervisory eye on "independent" labor relations agencies to a far greater degree than his predecessors. For the unions—to say nothing of management—were never content with "labor's voice" when they wanted to deal seriously with the administration. An Arthur Goldberg is the only sort of "unionist" who could sustain and broaden this reorientation; otherwise, reversion to traditional selection risks the new usefulness of this department. Other examples could be offered: Treasury, for one, has often been a drag on State and Defense, in part because of the traditional orientation of its secretary. . . .

Third is the effect on long-run organizational objectives—and options—inherent in the personalities and interests of particular appointees. The case of CEA has already been mentioned; so have the cases of State, the [national] security assistant, and the science adviser. Another example is the Budget Bureau. One more cost-accountant in the place would finish it off as a useful source of staff work for the President. Especially in the sphere of national security, the personalities and interests of initial appointees at State, Defense, Budget, and Treasury will go far to decide what can and cannot be done hereafter by way of improving "national policy machinery."

7. Organizing for Appointments below Cabinet Rank

This is an area in which the President-elect and his whole staff could easily get bogged down at no profit to themselves. For self-protection, three things should be done soon after Election Day:

First, an able, sensitive "personnel consultant" should be attached to the staff of the President-elect. This man should be an identified Democrat, known to have the confidence of both Kennedy and the [Democratic] National Committee chairman. . . . He should be designated as the clearinghouse for proposals on new presidential appointees, gripes against incumbents, shifts of personnel in Schedule C [positions]. He should master the schedule of expiring and new appointments, both Republican and Democratic, and be prepared with recommendations as these occur. He should master Schedule C [positions] on a government-wide basis and be prepared with replacements from within the career service, as appropriate.

Second, Roger Jones, the present chairman of the Civil Service Commission, should be designated for reappointment as chairman and requested to backstop this consultant, give him staff assistance (and do the detail work). Jones is a Republican appointee. One may not want to keep him on as chairman very long. Since the term of the other Republican member expires in February, a new man could be brought in and subsequently made chairman. But the advantage of having Jones at work as a backstopper, with a vote of confidence sufficient for the transition period, outweighs anything that could be gained from his removal in the short run.

Third, word should be passed to incoming department and agency heads that they will make nothing but trouble for themselves and the administration by unselective replacements or massive importations of persons at assistant secretary level and below. Changes should be made selectively and at leisure, using the guideline, "Know who your replacement is before you make a change."

It is no accident that in 1953 the two most effective officers in the first weeks after Inauguration Day [for Eisenhower] were [Joseph] Dodge at Budget and [George] Humphrey at Treasury. These were the two agencies where there was no "purging" and where inherited staffs were told they would be treated as reliable until they turned out otherwise. Humphrey and Dodge were immediately effective because they immediately had staffs at work behind them. For a Kennedy administration with the "Hundred Days" problem to lick, the lesson is obvious.

8. Reassuring the Bureaucracy

If one means to take the three steps suggested in #7 above ["Organizing for Appointments below Cabinet Rank"], one ought to get a maximum of credit for them from the bureaucracy. This calls for an early public statement to the effect that government careerists are a national resource and will be treated as such by the new regime. The reality of that intention will be demonstrated as those steps are taken. It will be demonstrated further if the working groups suggested in #2 above ["Organizing for a First Message to Congress"] begin, informally, to draw upon the expertise of selected bureaucrats long before Inauguration Day.

The more career officials can look forward to January 20 with hopeful, interested, even excited anticipation, the better the new administration will be served in the weeks after. To instill negative anticipation is to cut off one's own nose to spite one's face. That was the effect in 1953.

9. Consulting with the Legislative Leadership

From Election Day on, several things should be kept in mind:

(a) The Vice President–elect will be looking for work.

(b) In 1949, the new Senate leader was chosen by the Democrats just before Congress met, with the proviso that [Vice President Alben] Barkley keep the post until January 20. Is this precedent to be followed in 1961?

(c) Congress meets two weeks before inaugural; the committee chairmen—the same faces as before—will be looking for the "customary" laundry-list of presidential proposals in every sphere; in 1949, that custom helped to dissipate Truman's honeymoon. They also will be thinking about going into business for themselves; some of them will be doing it. Finally, they will be touchily awaiting signs of recognition from the President-elect . . .

(d) Congressional leaders will have to be consulted on, or at least informed of, the President-elect's immediate legislative plans. Their help will be needed in considering—and above all in sustaining—priorities. But consultation with whom, how, above all when? These questions will not necessarily look the same from the executive side as from the Senate.

(e) The first formal meeting with the legislative leaders, whether before or after Inauguration Day, will tend to set the form, tone, membership, and timing of future meetings. What purposes are these meetings to serve? Are they to be intimate sessions, à la FDR, or ambassadorial encounters, à la Eisenhower, with staffs present and minutes taken? Each of these points needs thought and a formulated approach by the President-elect.

10. Giving Congress Items before the First Message

Hopefully, some noncontroversial, simple, quick-action items could be introduced before Inauguration Day "on the President-elect's behalf," to "facilitate the work of the new administration." Within reason, the more of these the better, and the wider their spread across committees the better. One such item might be renewal of reorganization powers. . . . Other items may be found on the list of expiring legislation that the Budget Bureau will have ready, as a matter of routine, right after election. Uncovering such items and appraising their suitability could be a side job for the message "bird-dog" and the working groups suggested in #2 above ["Organizing for a First Message to Congress"].

11. Establishing Liaison with the Eisenhower Administration

There seems to be no need for "general" liaison and no point in assigning anyone to do that meaningless job. Presumably, Eisenhower will suggest a courtesy meeting and briefing, as Truman did in 1952, and will offer assistance toward a smooth transition. If he does not offer, he could be asked. Once the offer is made (or extorted), it should be used to establish several specific liaison arrangements. These include:

(a) Access for the President-elect to all government intelligence sources and for the prospective secretary of state to all the cable traffic he may want to see.

(b) Arrangements with the FBI for prompt security clearance of appointees.

(c) Access for a reliable associate of the prospective budget director to all aspects of the Budget Bureau's work in preparing the 1962 budget and in clearing legislation before January 20.

This should be for the purpose of obtaining information, not participating in decisions.

(d) Arrangements for use of Civil Service Commission staff and facilities, and for information on expiring appointments in the hands of the White House executive clerk.

(e) Arrangements for consultation by incoming officials with their outgoing opposite numbers and with departmental staffs. No limitations should be accepted on the freedom to inquire and consult.

(f) Arrangements for taking over White House offices and budget. It may turn out that the international or economic situation requires more than a courtesy consultation between Eisenhower and Kennedy; if so, the situation should be met as it deserves, with the proviso that Kennedy need make none of Eisenhower's decisions or accept commitments carrying past January 20. This proviso cannot be a prohibition; the situation may be unprecedented.

The President-elect must be prepared for a variety of international complications before inaugural. . . .

12. Organizing for Reorganizing

Not long after Election Day, it would be well to designate the members of the President's Advisory Committee on Government Organization. This is a three-man body created by Eisenhower as a part-time consultative group without staff of its own. Milton Eisenhower, Arthur Flemming, and Don Price are members. Price might be redesignated and the other two members drawn from among Kennedy appointees in other posts, or from academic circles. Whatever their other duties, all members should have government experience, a degree of detachment, strong sympathy for Kennedy, and be Democrats. Their task is to offer practical advice on a relatively intimate basis.

There are two reasons for designating this group early:

First, it is valuable to have a respectable place where Kennedy can refer—and defer—organizational proposals from the outgoing regime, from incoming cabinet members, and from elsewhere, until and unless he has time and resources to deal with them. There will be quantities of such proposals.

Second, there may well be some things he will want thought through for early action after inaugural, using reorganization powers (if available) or legislation. Several such reorganization possibilities exist: enough to keep an advisory committee busy from November.

13. Setting Ground Rules for Press Conferences

The big "press-radio-TV," televised press conference is a recent innovation; it serves some purposes well, others badly. It does not accomplish some of the objectives served by the quite different institution of Roosevelt's time. Whether any changes should or could be made is an open question. It is a question worth pursuing with responsible journalists. . . . If changes are intended, they should be instituted at the outset; the first press conference after inaugural will set a pattern hard to break.

14. Installing the "Shadow Government" in Washington

Very soon after Election Day, the President-elect will want to decide how fast and how formally—and in what facilities at whose expense—he wants his staff and cabinet designees, and ad hoc working groups in Washington.

This automatically involves decision also on the timing of vacations and of reconnaissance trips abroad by presidential designees, or by the President-elect. Shall they (or he) survey the free world? And when must they be back?

15. Preparing the Inaugural Address

It would be well not to begin this too early, but instead to wait until the main lines of a first message—that is to say of an initial program—had emerged. The inaugural address has to be a tone-setter. It will help to have a notion of what is to follow before spending much time on this introduction. It will also help to wait until one knows what international and economic conditions to expect by January 20.

16. Arranging the Physical Takeover

A number of troublesome details will have to be attended to. Some of them are unlikely to be settled without reference to the President-elect. These include:

(a) Arranging White House office space and Executive Office Building space.

(b) Determining what physical changes (temporary partitions and the like) have been made in the White House offices and at Old State, and deciding what the Eisenhower people should be asked to undo before January 20. (This is more serious than it may seem.)

(c) Deciding what personal facilities traditionally available for the President should be in readiness by January 20 and requesting that appropriate arrangements be made. These facilities include: automobiles, helicopters, planes, Shangri-La (now Camp David), two motor cruisers, and the yacht (in moth balls since 1953).

(d) Deciding on arrangements for inauguration ceremony, inaugural parade, and inaugural balls. Arrangements include invitation lists and tickets. Would Kennedy rather dispense with some "festivities"?

17. Arranging Initial Cabinet and NSC Meetings

Eisenhower surrounded these meetings with elaborate paperwork and preparatory consultations. Staffs have been created in each department to assist with preparations and follow-up. Also, cabinet meetings now include more presidential aides than department heads. Somewhat the same thing occurs in NSC meetings.

It is important that none of these procedures and arrangements continues, except as Kennedy specifically desires, after a chance to get his own feel for the uses of cabinet and NSC. Yet, the first meetings of these bodies could automatically perpetuate all sorts of Eisenhower practices. Past procedures will be carried on by career staffs unless they are deliberately interrupted.

It would be well, therefore, to confine early cabinet meetings to department heads of cabinet rank, along with the President's executive assistant, and to have only such agenda as the President may choose in consultation with his personal staff. As for initial NSC meetings, it would be well to confine them to statutory members, perhaps adding the budget director and the executive assistant, while the NSC secretary stuck to "secretarial" service, with agendas chosen by the President. (If either body were to take up issues involved in the first message, or impending budget amendments, he would probably want his message "bird-dog" in attendance.)

18. Program Development after Inauguration

Presumably the first message will not have been completed, or all fights on it finished, by January 20. This will remain to be put into final form. As that is done, attention would shift to amending Eisenhower's budget, the next great action with a deadline attached around which to organize administration planning and decisions. At the same time, it will be desirable to get study groups working, in or out of government, on desirable projects and programs, administrative and legislative, which are not to be, or cannot be, acted upon immediately.

These three steps—completing the first message, amending the budget, getting longer-range studies started—will be major items of concern for the President's first weeks in office. They represent, really, a late stage in "transition."

Like everything before, this stage should be set in awareness of possible complications from abroad.

Memo 2
Staffing the President-Elect

For: Senator John F. Kennedy
October 30, 1960

Summary

This memorandum makes proposals for initial staffing of the work you have to do in the first weeks after election. These proposals deal, specifically, with staff to meet your daily needs, to get started on your January program, to get moving on your personnel selections, and to help you plan next steps. Proposals are grouped by categories: continuing jobs (six), temporary jobs (ten or more), jobs for incumbents (five), jobs to defer (many). One job is in a special category: the budget directorship. This is not a scheme for White House and Executive Office organization. It is a start which can evolve into a scheme with the least risk of premature commitment on your part.

A President's needs for staff are bound to be different in many ways from a senator's or even from a candidate's. But your needs in the Presidency will also differ from Eisenhower's. Many of the needs and many of the differences cannot be fully understood, or met, until they have been experienced. They cannot be experienced until after January 20. The period before Inauguration Day is thus a time for caution.

In the next two weeks, however, you will have to staff yourself as President-elect, and the way you do so will affect what can be done thereafter. The staff you put together now, in the days after election, must be regarded as the core of your official staff, at least during your early months in office. It is trouble enough to build a staff group for the President-elect out of a campaign organization. It would be a waste of time—and you won't have the time—to shake your organization up again as you cease being President-elect and become President.

Some Things to Keep in Mind

In building a staff for the transition period, four rules of thumb are indicated:

First, define in your own mind the staff jobs for which you feel a concrete, immediate need in the weeks ahead. I have indicated below what I think these are. I have tried to be conservative. You may see more than I do. On the other hand, you may be unconvinced about the need for some of them. If so, do not let me or anyone talk you into anything. Wait until your own feel for your own situation validates or falsifies the needs we claim you have.

Presidential staffs have evolved in the last twenty years to meet two kinds of needs: on the one hand, needs of Presidents themselves, for help in managing their daily chores, in gaining information, and in keeping control of key government decisions; on the other hand, needs of other government officials for backing, support, judgment, or decision, or a borrowing of prestige from the President. At this stage, I urge you to consider only needs of the first sort—your own. There will be plenty of people thinking about how you should be staffed in order to help them. You are the only person you can count on to be thinking about what helps you.

Second, as among the jobs you see you need, decide provisionally which ones are clearly continuing, bound to persist into your Presidency because foreseeable needs after January 20 are so much like the needs you face right now. Announce prospective government positions only for the men you put into these jobs. If you are uncertain about continuation (or about the man), or if a job is clearly temporary, treat it as a "consultantship," without long-term commitment and without a government title.

Third, think through the titles you intend for your continuing staff jobs, with reference to the work you have in mind and for the bureaucratic or public connotation of titles used by Eisenhower. The men whom you appoint now and intend to keep with you when you take office will be very much advantaged in their work during the interim if they are publicly identified quite early as prospective members of your presidential staff. But the titles you announce for them should suggest what you expect of them and, more important, should not suggest what you do not expect. Any title now in use by Eisenhower may attract a lot of "customary" business that you actually want handled somewhere else, or not at all, or on which you prefer experimentation. Such a title also may connote a ranking in your staff that you do not intend, or do not want to freeze; Adams's title "*the* assistant to the President" is a notable example. . . .

Fourth, before you appoint anyone to anything, give some thought to the kinds of relationships you want, initially, among the jobs you need, and hence among the men who fill them, with regard to one another and to you. The interim staff that I suggest below is closer to Roosevelt's pattern than to Eisenhower's: You would be your own "chief of staff." Your chief assistants would have to work collegially, in constant touch with one another and with you. Their respective jobs are demarcated by distinctly separable main assignments, so that they need not flounder, or dash off in all directions, or fall over one another. But these are activity assignments, in terms of what you have to do from day to day, not programmatic assignments to marked-off policy areas. Since your activities overlap, these jobs will overlap; no one's jurisdiction is exclusive; competition is built in. There is room here for a *primus inter pares* to emerge, but no room for a staff director or arbiter, short of you. Neither is there room for sheer, unguided struggle. Jurisdictions are distinguished as well as overlapped.

Is that what you want when you become President? If so, your interim appointments and assignments must contribute toward it; if not, they must contribute to preventing it.

This is a crucial choice. For if you follow my advice, you will commit yourself not to each detail of Rooseveltian practice—some details are out of date, others were unfortunate—but to the spirit of his presidential operation; whereby you would oversee, coordinate, and interfere with virtually everything your staff was doing. A collegial staff has to be managed; competition has to be audited. To run a staff in Roosevelt's style imposes heavy burdens. He himself dropped some of them during the war. Eisenhower, clearly, could not have endured them for a moment. Truman, though his practice somewhat followed FDR's, never fully understood what half his staff was doing; thus, he escaped part of the load.

But if the burdens are heavy, the rewards are great. No one has yet improved on Roosevelt's relative success at getting information in his mind and key decisions in his hands reliably enough and soon enough to give him room for maneuver. That, after all, is (or ought to be) the aim of presidential staff work.

As you weigh this choice, you may want to consider the ideas (or instincts) that underlay Rooseveltian practice. Accordingly, I have appended to this memorandum a description of the FDR approach to White House staffing (Attachment A), and another on his approach to the Budget (Attachment B).

Continuing Jobs to Be Filled at Once

I recommend that immediately after election you proceed to define and fill the following jobs, with the understanding that the men selected will take office with you as the core of your continuing staff.

(1) An Assistant for Program. In terms of your ability to make a fast start and firm impression on the country and on Congress after January 20, here is the key staff appointment before you. This is the "program aide" or "message bird-dog" mentioned in my memorandum of September 15.

Before inaugural, his task would be threefold:

(a) To help you organize the consultations, working groups, drafting teams, etc., that you may find you need in order to fill gaps, to reconsider, to refine, and to prepare your initial legislative program and a complementary program of executive action.

(b) To help prepare your inaugural address, in light of and in coordination with these program preparations.

(c) To ride herd, in your name and as your agent, on the work thus set in motion, in order to define and sharpen issues for decision and in order to ensure the readiness of necessary action documents—messages, bill drafts, statements, executive orders—by the due-date you intend for your first program presentation.

This assumes that you will want to go to Congress very early with priority requests, a rationale for your priorities, and a showing of executive activity to boot.

Inauguration Day would find this aide at work completing preparations for that early presentation. Thereafter, he could readily become your principal assistant in preparing or reviewing the endless stream of public documents—messages, speeches, statements, orders, bill drafts, budget amendments—through which you will continue to define and to defend your personal program. With this continuing assignment he would tend to be, and should have scope to be, a focal point for general-purpose staff work in the White House on policy development in every sphere, legislative and administrative, foreign and domestic.

The continuing program job, as thus described, bears a close family resemblance to the job that [Samuel] Rosenman did for Roosevelt as his "special counsel" or that [Clark] Clifford and then [Charles] Murphy did for Truman, under the same title. (The title suited the man, not vice versa; all three happened to be lawyers.) If the job is to be done with maximum effectiveness, it should encompass all the public documents which bear upon your program. At the same time, it should be quite clear that dealing with documents means coming to grips with substance, and dealing with public documents requires knowledge of the private ones. This is not per se a writer's job, and it is not per se an attorney's job. Nor is it a job to be walled off from any area of program-making or of policy concern, not even from the area of highest security classification. The man on whom you will rely to help you state your program must have a feel for every part of it, including what cannot be stated.

In Truman's time, the special counsel's job was thought to be primarily "domestic" in orientation. Clifford and Murphy got deep into the substance of domestic policy; they rarely ventured far into the substance of foreign or military policy, though Murphy sometimes did so during the Korean War. But this weighting on the domestic side was a hangover from the days when national security affairs were outside the mainstream of government concerns except in "emergencies." Nowadays these affairs *are* the mainstream, and "emergencies" are commonplace. In your administration such a program aide cannot be thought of as primarily "domestic." His policy concerns should match your own. His qualifications should be judged accordingly.

This does not mean that he can be a second secretary of state (any more than he can be a second secretary of interior). The program aide has got to shift from problem to problem and policy to policy depending on the speech you next have to deliver or the executive order you next must sign. His priorities are set by your priorities. He shifts a step before you do. He has to be as much a generalist as you, no less concerned with substance but no more able to dwell for long on any given subject.

Above all else this aide should have a mind and working habits that fit yours. You cannot get good service of this sort at arm's length, either intellectually or personally.

Once you choose your program aide, there will be need to organize some temporary staffing and consultative arrangements necessary for initial program preparation before January 20. The most urgent of these are sketched below [in the section "Temporary Jobs to Fill Soon"]. The whole subject of producing your first program will be treated in a later memorandum.

(2) A Personal Assistant to the Commander-in-Chief–Elect. This job relates to relatively new activities incumbent on a President by virtue of the weapons revolution in a cold war context. Immediately after the election you should have a man on your own staff, constantly in touch with you, always within reach, to do four things:

(a) To brief you and your closest personal assistants on the responsibility that will be yours, as commander-in-chief, on and after January 20, for special categories of reversible and irreversible decisions. Should Eisenhower be confronted with certain of these decisions before Inauguration Day, he might feel impelled to consult you. You might feel impelled to respond. You cannot wait until then to be briefed.

(b) To brief you and your close aides, in detail, on present arrangements for arriving at and implementing such decisions, and to give you a complete appraisal of the strengths and weaknesses built into these arrangements including intelligence aspects.

(c) To brief you and your close aides on the facts, the inferences, and the discrepancies which are built into Eisenhower's program (and budget) assumptions, and on data pertinent to judgment of appropriate assumptions for developing your program.

(d) To be your personal eyes and ears in the intelligence agencies of government, drawing your attention to raw data that you ought to see and to especially able specialists, at whatever levels, whom you ought to meet. This is not a "liaison" task in the sense of passive channel, but a personal assistantship in the sense of active auditing for you.

These things roughly correspond to (and expand upon) the work now done for Eisenhower by General [Andrew] Goodpaster, on a special assignment over and above his publicized job as White House Staff secretary. Your man should be in touch with Goodpaster before inauguration and should carry on with you thereafter. Even at the outset he should be more than a Goodpaster; more an assistant than a channel and alert to every facet of your interest and your work. He needs to be curious, sensitive, independent, and as knowledgeable about policy as about intelligence.

The quickest way to get your hands on such a man is to request that someone now cleared, qualified, and in the government be detailed to you for temporary assignment. This has the additional advantage of committing you to nothing in the way of permanent arrangements. . . .

(3) An Assistant for Press Relations. From the moment you are President-elect you acquire many of the public relations risks and opportunities inherent in the Presidency. Everything you say or do will be watched and weighed, at home and abroad—not by the press alone, or by the public, but by officialdom.

Therefore, you have immediate need for both types of assistance traditionally expected from a President's press secretary:

First, the "outside" job of acting as your spokesman to the press and as housemother or hand-holder for White House correspondents. Second, the "inside" job of counseling on public relations aspects of your actions and statements day by day—a job which brings him into everybody's business, especially the program aide's.

These two types of assistance are *not* easily combined in one man. They tend to pull in opposite directions; they call for rather different skills and temperaments; the man who tries to do them both is under constant strain. No one is likely to do both equally well.

To meet your needs for both becomes a tricky proposition. Before you choose a man as your continuing chief press aide, you will want to decide which of these jobs you expect him to stress and how you mean to buttress his performance of the other.

If you do not want to cross this bridge at once, you could meet momentary needs by carrying your present [campaign] press relations organization into the transition period. But if your designations are *pro tem,* the men involved must know it; so must the working press. For obvious reasons, such a holding operation grows less satisfactory with each passing week; it probably becomes intolerable by early January.

(4) Two Assistants for Operations. Immediately after election you will need at least two men dividing up assorted daily chores:

(a) Arranging your schedule, marshaling visitors, guarding your door. For a time, your personal secretary could keep up with this. But after you are settled down and vulnerable in Washington it almost certainly will become too much for her.

(b) Managing your temporary office operation; superintending physical arrangements (and financing), keeping tabs on clerical assistance and on correspondence, handling preliminaries to the takeover of White House facilities and funds. (This sounds like "office-management," but such work at your level has plenty of political and policy content.)

(c) Superintending preparations for your trip abroad (if any): physical arrangements, briefings, communications services, etc.

(d) Arranging for FBI clearances of your appointees and Secret Service clearances of designees for White House passes.

(e) Keeping tabs on and facilitating contacts by your other aides with outgoing officials at the White House and elsewhere.

(f) Following up commitments you have made to visitors, and keeping track of their performance on commitments made to you. This includes tactful follow-up of ad hoc jobs you have assigned to temporary aides (see below).

(g) Watching for noncompliance with the orders you have given (in the few spheres where a President-elect gives orders), identifying blockages, and intervening at your option.

(h) Watching for and helping to unravel snarls in the evolving personal relations among those who are prospectively in your official family.

(i) Standing in at meetings you prefer to duck and "studying" proposals you want sat on.

These are the chores of daily operations, not as they will manifest themselves when you take office, but as they will start to look by mid-November. Even at this early stage one can identify, in embryo, the separate jobs of an "appointments secretary," of a "staff secretary," of a possible "assistant to the President," and of several "administrative assistants" on ad hoc assignments.

But for the moment two men should suffice, with help from your personal secretary and (as needed) from such temporary aides or volunteers as you find wise. You can suspend judgment, for the time being, on the numbers (and the titles) ultimately needed when you shift from being President-elect to being President.

You may want to treat this bundle of assignments not as two jobs (and later more) for different men, but as one job for one man with a growing number of assistants: the "number-one boy for general operations" projected in my memorandum of September 15. However, on reflection, I would urge you to go slow. My "number-one boy" can begin as two and become three or four; depending on the personalities involved, he may emerge through "natural selection" if you let him. But you may decide to operate without him. January would be time enough for a decision. By then you will know more about the White House as now organized and more about your own future requirements.

(5) A Personal Secretary. For the time being you can proceed with the secretarial arrangements you found suitable as a senator. By sometime in December, however (depending on your travel plans), your personal workload is likely to confront you with a choice which you will have to face in any event when you take office: do you want your present personal secretary to be just that . . . or do you want her involved permanently with "operations" chores, such as your daily schedule? If you find that you have something of the latter sort in mind, you will want to save an appropriate title for her and will want to cast about for someone else to handle your dictation and your private files.

Temporary Jobs to Fill Soon

I recommend that before Thanksgiving you begin to fill the following jobs, with the understanding that these are transition assignments, involving no long-run commitment to job content or to men.

(1) A Consultant on Personnel. Selection of political appointees at subcabinet level and in Schedule C positions could be an area in which you and your whole staff get bogged down at no profit to yourselves. Therefore, as soon as possible after election, you will have use for an interim consultant working quietly for you on these appointments. His work would include:

(a) Identifying very able men, in private life and government, whom you should know but do not, and arranging that you have an early look at them for future reference.

(b) Seeking talent for specific jobs in which you have an interest and checking talents of those urged on you by others.

(c) Checking the proposals of cabinet designees for such of their assistants as are subject to your appointment, with an eye to your interest and your protection.

(d) Mastering the schedule of expiring term appointments, both Republican and Democratic, in the regulatory commissions and working with a special study group (see below) on standards for replacements. (The list of expiration dates is in the hands of the White House executive clerk.)

(e) Mastering the policy jobs in Schedule C, government-wide, and keeping a watchful eye on what your cabinet designees intend—again, in your interest and for your protection. The chairman of the Civil Service Commission can provide assistance here (see below).

(f) Serving as a clearinghouse and checkpoint for talent searches (in and out of government) that cabinet designees themselves get underway.

(g) Serving as your personal adviser on relations with and policies regarding the career services.

The man who does this should be "high-level," sophisticated in government, alert and sensitive to policy, well versed in the "who is where" of business and the professions, knowledgeable about personnel techniques but not a "personnel man," knowledgeable about politics but not a politician (though certainly a Democrat). The foundations are the likeliest source of such a man. . . .

(2) A Liaison with the National Committee. Your personnel consultant cannot be your man "out front" on political appointments. For his protection and survival—and for your own purposes—you need somebody else to take the heat, pass the word, fend off the importunate, and soothe the disappointed. I am not concerned now with middle- and low-level patronage jobs—that heat can be contained in the committee for awhile—but with high-prestige appointments, where the heat will be immediate, intense, and on you.

(3) A Consultant on Organization. Soon after election you will need to start identifying and appraising "next steps" for the later stages of transition in December, January, and February. Much of this work will be done, in the normal course, by your permanent assistants from the moment you appoint them. But you and they together could use at least one interim consultant on the mysteries and choices you all face in organizing and operating the White House Office and the Executive Office. Depending on your current intentions, you may have use for him, as well, in working out immediate reorganization plans for other areas of government. . . .

By some time in December you could also use a small group of advisers in the organization field to serve as a respectable repository for reorganization schemes urged on you from outside, until you have the time and resources to deal with them. For this purpose you might want to name three men as prospective members of the President's Advisory Committee on Government Organization. Your interim consultant might (or might not) serve as one of these advisers, but his short-run task is not the same as theirs. He deals with your immediate needs; they deal with large-scale questions for the future.

(4) A Liaison with the Budget Bureau. At the earliest opportunity, you should put a man inside the Budget Bureau as a close observer (not participant) of budget preparation, legislative clearances, and staff performance. Until you name a prospective budget director (see below) this liaison man should be in close touch with your program aide; afterwards, he should assist them both. His job is not the same as the prospective director's. . . .

(5) Assistants for Ad Hoc Assignments. As you feel the need, you will want to take on temporary aides for ad hoc troubleshooting and fact-finding jobs, both on your own behalf and in connection with the rapidly evolving work of your program aide. But as a general rule: do not add to your own staff more of these odd-job men than you can use and supervise. And do not let your program aide have more men answering to him than he can keep under his thumb from day to day.

(6) Working Groups on Programs. There will be some problem areas where you and your program assistant find it necessary or expedient to use a group instead of single aides in the preliminary work of screening ideas, sharpening issues, posing choices, and then actually turning out draft action documents.

For example, in the national security area, a working-level version of the present [Paul] Nitze group is probably essential both to substitute for departmental staffs and to consult with them on your behalf, and on behalf of your department heads (who will have no departments).

Another example is the economic-fiscal area, where no one man could cope with sorting out and bringing down to earth the cloudy mass of conflicting advice you will receive from every part of the economy, to say nothing of academia. Unless I miss my guess, you and your program aide will need a select, "back-room" group of practical, adroit, low-ego lawyers and economists—or maybe several groups in different areas—to deal with this.

(7) Contact Men with Advisory Groups. I hate to think that you might have to set up and then live with formal, consultative groups of prominent persons in private life. However, in at least one area—fiscal-monetary policy—it is conceivable that this could become necessary for symbolic purposes, if better symbols (like a Treasury appointment) had to be deferred or seemed unwise.

Should any such groups be created, it will be imperative to keep them from swamping your evolving organization for program preparation. To protect your program aide and his associates from continual interruption and diversion, you will need special, temporary aides as buffers, arrangers, hand-holders, and spies upon whatever formal, outside groups you may bring into being.

(8) A Study Group on Regulatory Appointments. The regulatory commissions are in such a bad way (by and large) and appointments have been so mishandled under two administrations that it would be well to set these posts aside, while a sophisticated study group (not necessarily publicized) considers standards for recruitment and selection of commissioners. . . . Your attorney general should be drawn in when appointed. Your personnel consultant should be kept in touch. You may want advice from still other sources. But before you let a single commissionership into your appointments process, you should bear in mind precisely how you plan to treat them all.

Jobs to Be Done by Incumbents

I recommend that in whatever sequence suits the cause of good publicity you announce your intention to reappoint the following incumbent officials. This is not an exhaustive list; it is an immediate one.

Your long-run plans for any of these men (and their positions) are not cramped by such announcements. Commitments of this sort need not bind you to them for very long. In the short-run, your intention gives you claims upon their services, even while they are Eisenhower's subordinates. This would be useful to you and them.

These announcements also serve some useful purposes in terms of public and personnel relations.

(1) Director of CIA. The usefulness of short-run stability and service here is obvious, particularly since you would not be dependent on the agency for personal assistance. Your C-in-C assistant gives you that (see above).

(2) Executive Secretary of NSC. [The incumbent] regards himself as a careerist, having held the job since 1949. It is useful to confirm him in this view (for the time being, anyway). Your programmers may want historical details and data he could readily provide. You will want to take a careful look at NSC machinery and avoid a premature commitment to procedures; he can run it on a basis which protects you from commitments (if you tell him to). He also can be useful as a temporary channel to and from all sorts of persons in the bowels of the bureaucracy.

(3) "Science Adviser" to the President. His title, technically, is special assistant for science and technology; he also serves as chairman of the President's Science Advisory Committee. You will want easy access to the men who have been dealing from inside with current government concerns and controversies. This is a way to ensure it; it also insures you against premature commitments to particular advisers or machinery. . . .

(4) Chairman of the Civil Service Commission. [The incumbent] is a distinguished careerist (nominally Republican) who served Roosevelt and Truman before Eisenhower. Since there will be a Democratic vacancy in the commission in March, you could replace him as chairman rather shortly if you chose. But in the interim, to give him status as your chairman is to free him for a wide variety of useful work in servicing and backstopping your personnel consultant. With respect to the whole realm of Schedule C, [his] technical assistance, contacts, savvy would be very valuable. But they could not be readily available if he were confined to the role of "Eisenhower's man."

(5) Director of the FBI. [The incumbent's] reappointment seems a matter of course; you might as well make the most of it by an early announcement, particularly since you may well find some things you would like him to do for you, quite confidentially, before Inauguration.

A Prospective Budget Director

As a presidential staff facility, at one remove from personal aides, the Budget Bureau is not what it used to be (and rarely was what it ought to be). But it is still the nearest thing to institutional eyes-and-ears and memory, encompassing all parts of the executive branch, which you will have available to you when you take office.

You are almost sure to find (as Roosevelt, Truman, Eisenhower did before you) that when you look down from on high, the Budget Bureau seems a better and more valuable institution than it appears in the eyes of departmental staffs, of congressmen, or even its own critics from within. It looks better to Presidents because they find they cannot do without it; others can.

If you are to make the most of this facility—both in the short-run terms of your initial budgeting and in the longer terms of general staff work—your budget director needs to be a different sort of man from Eisenhower's appointees, or for that matter, Truman's. Eisenhower had a penchant for certified public accountants. You need a man who is soaked in substance, a broad-gauged policy adviser, not an accountant.

At the same time your man should have real sensitivity to the requirements and limits of staff work in an "institutional" staff role. You do not want him dominated by your cabinet officers, but neither do you want him thinking he is one of them, or above them. You are above them; he is merely staff to you. Yet this does not mean that you should give him, or that he should seek, the status of a purely personal adviser. You want your White House aides to think in terms of you. You want this man to think more nearly of the Presidency. You then preserve some freedom to select between the two or interweave them. Your budget director needs the sensitivity to see this from the start.

He also needs toughness (preferably under a bland exterior). The core jobs of his agency are budget preparation and legislative clearance. By their nature he becomes a chief "no" man for you. Far more than congressmen or bureaucrats believe, past Presidents have instigated and supported bureau negatives.

But the reason why your man ought to be program-minded, not a cost accountant, is that national or presidential needs may call on him to urge you to say "yes." . . . Even as early as December he could be extremely useful:

(a) Working in tandem with your program aide on the substance of issues, and preparing for follow-up on budgetary or administrative aspects of the concrete program choices you will make.

(b) Serving as a critic of those choices, bringing independent views to bear for your consideration.

(c) Serving also as a source of counsel and critique on the work of your personnel and organization consultants.

(d) Arranging for and superintending temporary liaison with departmental staffs where you have deferred top appointments, or where your appointees delay liaison on their own.

(e) Serving, temporarily, as liaison with second-level, special-purpose staffs now in or near the White House, which you probably will want to liquidate, but meanwhile need to freeze. . . .

Concluding Note

My recommendations are highly academic in the sense that they take no account of given personalities, or mental sets, or skills, or work habits including yours. Even if you see the need for jobs suggested here, and even if you like my general scheme, the moment you begin to put men into jobs there will be need for review, perhaps for readjustment, of the duties and relationships I now propose. The review should be by you, and but the first of many in the months ahead. This brings me back to my starting point: once you are "Mr. President," nobody else can fully gauge your own, personal interests. In the last analysis, that is the "staff job" for you.

Memo 2
Attachment A: Roosevelt's Approach to Staffing the White House

For: Senator John F. Kennedy
October 30, 1960

Reorganization Plan I of 1939, which created a "White House Office" and distinguished it from the rest of the "Executive Office of the President," marks the start of modern presidential staffing. What Roosevelt did, in practice, with the institutions then established shows him at his most relevant for the contemporary Presidency. Relatively speaking, in terms of presidential organization, the immediate prewar years have more kinship with 1961 than do the crisis years of the depression (or the years after Pearl Harbor, for that matter).

Roosevelt did not theorize about "operating principles," but he evidently had some, for his practice was remarkably consistent in essentials. His "principles" can be deduced from what he did and from the memories of men around him, as follows.

1. White House Staff as Personal Staff

The White House was his house, his home as well as office. No one was to work there who was not essential for the conduct of his own work, day by day. "This is the White House calling" was to mean him, or somebody acting intimately and immediately for him. The things he personally did not do from week to week, the trouble-shooting and intelligence he did not need first-hand, were to be staffed outside the White House. The aides he did not have to see from day to day were to be housed in other offices than his. This is the origin of the distinction which developed in his time between "personal" and "institutional" staff. The Executive Office was conceived to be the place for "institutional" staff; the place, in other words, for everybody else.

2. Fixed Assignments to Activities Not Program Areas

Roosevelt had a strong sense of a cardinal fact in government: That Presidents don't act on policies, programs, or personnel in the abstract; they act in the concrete as they meet deadlines set by due dates—or the urgency—of documents awaiting signature, vacant posts awaiting appointees, officials seeking interviews, newsmen seeking answers, audiences waiting for a speech, intelligence reports requiring a response, etc., etc. He also had a strong sense of another fact in government: That persons close to Presidents are under constant pressure—and temptation—to go into business for themselves, the more so as the word gets out that they deal regularly with some portion of his business.

Accordingly, he gave a minimum of fixed assignments to the members of his personal staff. Those he did give out were usually in terms of helping him to handle some specific and recurrent stream of action-forcing deadlines he himself could not escape.

Thus, before the war, he had one aide regularly assigned to help him with his personal press relations and with those deadline-makes, his press conferences: the press secretary. Another aide was regularly assigned to schedule his appointments and to guard his door: the appointments secretary. Early in the war he drew together several scattered tasks and put them regularly in the hands of Samuel Rosenman as "special counsel." (The title was invented for the man; Rosenman, a lawyer and a judge, had held a similar title and done comparable work for FDR in Albany.) [His tasks included] pulling together drafts of presidential messages, speeches, and policy statements, reviewing proposed executive orders, administration bill drafts, and action on enrolled bills—in short, assisting with the preparation of all public documents through which Roosevelt defined and pressed his program.

These fixed assignments, and others like them in the Roosevelt staff, were activity assignments, not programmatic ones. They were organized around recurrent presidential obligations, not functional subject matters. They were differentiated by particular sorts of actions, not by particular program areas. This had three consequences:

(a) The men on such assignments were compelled to be generalists, jacks-of-all-trades, with a perspective almost as unspecialized as the President's own, cutting across every program area, every government agency, and every facet of his work, personal, political, legislative, administrative, ceremonial.

(b) Each assignment was distinct from others but bore a close relationship to others, since the assigned activities, themselves, were interlinked at many points. Naturally, the work of the press secretary and the special counsel overlapped, while both had reason for concern and for involvement, often enough, with the work of the appointments secretary—and so forth. These men knew what their jobs were, but they could not do them without watching, checking, jostling one another. Roosevelt liked it so.

(c) Since each man was a "generalist" in program terms, he could be used for ad hoc special checks and inquiries depending on the President's needs of the moment. So far as their regular work allowed, the fixed-assignment men were also general-utility trouble-shooters. No one was supposed to be too specialized for that.

3. Deliberate Gaps in Activity Assignments

There were some spheres of recurrent action, of activities incumbent on the President, where Roosevelt evidently thought it wise to have no staff with fixed, identified assignments. One was the sphere of his continuing relations with the leaders and members of Congress. Another was the sphere of his own choices for the chief appointive offices in his administration. A third was the sphere of his direct relations with department heads, both individually and as a cabinet. Every Roosevelt aide on fixed assignment was involved to some degree in all three spheres. These and other aides were always liable to be used, ad hoc, on concrete problems in these spheres. But no one save the President was licensed to concern himself exclusively, or continuously, with FDR's congressional relations, political appointments, or cabinet-level contacts.

4. General-Purpose Aides on Irregular Assignments

After 1939 and on into the war years, FDR had several "administrative assistants" on his personal staff, all of them conceived as "generalists," whom he could use, ad hoc, as chore-boys, troubleshooters, checker-uppers, intelligence operatives, and as magnets for ideas, gripes, gossip in the administration, on the Hill, and with groups outside government. These men were also used, as need arose, to backstop and assist the aides who did have fixed assignments.

FDR intended his administrative assistants to be eyes and ears and manpower for him, with no fixed contacts, clients, or involvements of their own to interfere when he had need to redeploy them. Naturally, these general-purpose aides gained know-how in particular subject matter areas, and the longer they worked on given ad hoc jobs the more they tended to become functional "specialists." One of them, David Niles, got so involved in dealings with minority groups that Truman kept him on with this as his fixed specialty. Roosevelt's usual response to such a situation would have been to shake it up before the specialization grew into a fixed assignment.

Roosevelt never wanted in his House more general-purpose men for ad hoc missions than he personally could supervise, direct, assign, and reassign. During the war, however, as his needs and interests changed, his White House staff inevitably tended to become a two-level operation, with some aides quite remote from his immediate concerns or daily supervision. How he might have met this tendency, after the war, we have no means of knowing.

5. Ad Hoc Staff Work by Outsiders

It never seems to have occurred to FDR that his only sources of such ad hoc personal assistance were the aides in his own office. He also used Executive Office aides, personal friends, idea-men or technicians down in the bureaucracy, old Navy hands, old New

York hands, experts from private life, cabinet officers, little cabinet officers, diplomats, relatives—especially his wife—as supplementary eyes and ears and manpower. He often used these "outsiders" to check or duplicate the work of White House staff, or to probe into spheres where the White House aides should not be seen, or to look into things he guessed his staff would be against.

He disliked to be tied to any single source of information or advice on anything. Even if the source should be a trusted aide, he preferred, when and where he could, to have alternative sources.

6. FDR as "Chief of Staff"

In Roosevelt's White House there was no place for a Sherman Adams. Roosevelt made and shifted the assignments; he was the recipient of staff work; he presided at the morning staff meetings; he audited the service he was getting; he coordinated A's report with B's (or if he did not, they went uncoordinated and he sometimes paid a price for that). Before the war, reportedly, he planned to keep one of his administrative assistants on tap "in the office," to "mind the shop" and be a sort of checker-upper on the others. But he never seems to have put this intention into practice. From time to time he did lean on one aide above all others in a given area. In wartime, for example, Harry Hopkins was distinctly *primus inter pares* on a range of vital matters for a period of time. But Hopkins's range was never as wide as the President's. And Hopkins's primacy was not fixed, codified, or enduring. It depended wholly on their personal relationship and Roosevelt's will. In certain periods their intimacy waxed; it also waned.

7. Wartime Innovations

From 1941 to 1943 Roosevelt brought new staff into the White House. Superficially, the new men and their new assignments made the place look different. But as he dealt with wartime staff, he operated very much as he had done before. He let his prewar pattern bend; despite appearances, he did not let it break.

The principal new arrivals were [Samuel] Rosenman, [Harry] Hopkins, [Admiral William] Leahy, a "Map Room," and [James] Byrnes. Rosenman, as special counsel, has already been mentioned. Hopkins evolved into a sort of super administrative assistant, working on assignments without fixed boundaries in the conduct of the wartime Grand Alliance, and collaborating with Rosenman on major speeches. Leahy, as chief of staff to the commander-in-chief, became an active channel to and from the services and kept an eye upon the White House Map Room. This was a reporting and communications center, staffed by military personnel, in direct touch with the services, with war fronts, with intelligence sources, and with allied governments. As for Byrnes, he left the Supreme Court to be a "deputy" for Roosevelt in resolving quarrels among the agencies concerned with war production and the war economy. Byrnes's assignment was relatively fixed, but limited, temporary, and entirely at the pleasure of the President, dependent on their personal relationship. In 1944, when Congress turned his job into a separate, statutory office (OWMR [Office of War Mobilization and Reconversion]), Byrnes hastened to resign.

The thing to note about these wartime aides is that none of them had irreversible assignments, or exclusive jurisdictions, or control over each other, or command over remaining members of the peacetime staff. Regarding all of them, and as he dealt with each of them, Roosevelt remained his own "chief of staff." And he continued to employ outsiders for assistance. Winston Churchill, among others, now became an alternative source.

8. Reliance on Others than Staff for Ideas

Wartime changes gave the White House staff much more involvement in, and more facilities for, program development than had been the case in 1939. But Roosevelt never seems to have conceived his personal staff—not even when enlarged by Rosenman, Hopkins, Byrnes—as the sole or even the main source of policy innovators and idea men. Ideas and innovations were supposed to flow from inside the departments, from the Hill, and from outside of government. His staff was meant to save them from suppression, give them air, and check them out, not to think them up. White House aides were certainly encouraged to have "happy thoughts," but they were not relied upon to be the chief producers. The same thing, incidentally, can be said of budget aides.

9. Operations to the Operators

FDR was always loath to let into his House routine activities, except where he chose otherwise for the time being. This seems to be one of the reasons (not the only one) why he never had "legislative liaison" assistants continuously working at the White House. Reportedly, he foresaw what has come to be the case in Eisenhower's time, that if the White House were routinely in the liaisoning business, congressmen and agencies alike would turn to his assistants for all sorts of routine services and help. "It is all your trouble, not mine," he once informed his cabinet officers, with reference to the bills that they were sponsoring. This was his attitude toward departmental operations generally, always excepting those things that he wanted for his own, or felt he had to grab because of personalities and circumstances.

10. Avoidance of Coordination by Committee

After experimenting elaborately in his first term, Roosevelt lost taste for interagency committees. Thereafter, he never seems to have regarded any of them—from the cabinet down—as a vehicle for doing anything that could be done by operating agencies or by a staff. This left small scope for such committees at his level. He used the cabinet as a sounding board, sometimes, and sometimes as a means to put his thinking, or his "magic," on display. Otherwise, his emphasis was on staffs and on operating agencies, taken one by one or in an ad hoc group.

11. The Budget Bureau as a Back-Up Staff

For routine, or preliminary, or depth staff work that his White House aides could not take on, Roosevelt usually looked to the Budget Bureau (or alternatively, to a man or group he trusted in the operating agencies). In many ways, the modern bureau was his personal creation; in most ways it has never been as near to full effectiveness as in his time. This aspect of Roosevelt's approach to staffing is the subject of Attachment B.

Memo 2
Attachment B: Roosevelt's Approach to Staffing the Budget Bureau

For: Senator John F. Kennedy
October 30, 1960

In Roosevelt's time, the Executive Office of the President was little else except the Bureau of the Budget. This agency had been in existence since 1921, housed in Treasury but reporting to the President as his source of staff assistance in preparing the executive budget. Under the Republicans, budgeting had been regarded very largely as a negative endeavor to squeeze departmental estimates. The bureau had been staffed accordingly. Its career staff was small, dull, conscientious, unimaginative. But by 1936, FDR's experience had made him sympathetic to the point of view expressed by his Committee on Administrative Management: that the budget process—as a stream of actions with deadlines attached—gave him unequalled opportunities to get his hands on key decisions about operating levels and forward plans in every part of the executive branch.

Accordingly, he set to work to revamp and restaff the Budget Bureau. In 1937 he made it the custodian of another action-forcing process: routine coordination in his name of agency draft bills, reports on pending bills, recommendations on enrolled bills, and proposed executive orders. This is the so-called legislative clearance function, involving both the substance and financing of proposals, which the bureau has continued ever since and which, since Rosenman's time, has been linked closely to the White House special counsel.

In 1939 Roosevelt moved the bureau from Treasury into his Executive Office. At the same time, he appointed a new budget director, Harold Smith, and backed a tenfold increase in the bureau's career staff. In the five years after 1937, the staff was built from 40 to 400, roughly to its present size. Smith's emphasis in staffing was threefold. First, he enlarged the number, raised the caliber, and cut the paperwork of budget analysts, the men who did detailed reviews of departmental budgets. Second, he brought in a separate group of organization and procedures men to look at departmental work in terms of managerial effectiveness, not sheer economy. Third, he began rather covertly to build another staff group with a still different perspective: program-oriented men, economists for the most part, to review departmental work in terms of policy effectiveness and to provide him special studies on short notice.

From Smith and from the staff that Smith was building, FDR sought service of three sorts: First, he wanted cool, detached appraisals of the financial, managerial, and program rationality in departmental budget plans and legislative programs. Second, he wanted comparable appraisals of the bright ideas originating in his own mind, or the minds of his political and personal associates. Third, he wanted the White House backstopped by preliminary and subsidiary staff work of the sort his own aides could not undertake without forfeiting their availability and flexibility as a small group of generalists on his immediate business.

All sorts of things now thought to call for special staffs or secretariats or interagency committees were once sought from the budget staff or from an ad hoc working group drawn out of the departments by some specialist inside that staff. The oldest "secretariat" now operating in the Presidency is the bureau's Office of Legislative Reference, which handles the clearance function. The precursors of Eisenhower's public works inventories, aviation surveys, foreign aid reviews, and the like were staff studies undertaken by the bureau in the 1940s.

Memo 3
Cabinet Departments: Some Things to Keep in Mind

For: Senator John F. Kennedy
November 3, 1960

In choosing cabinet officers and heads of major agencies you will want to consider the usual criteria of party, interest-group, and geographic "representativeness," and you will naturally have more personal matters in mind. These last are none of my business.

There are, however, certain additional factors which it will be worth your while to keep in mind. These bear upon your own ability as President to conserve your freedom of action and to guard your reputation. Your personal effectiveness in office will be influenced considerably by what the great departments can do for you or do to you. In turn the kinds of service—or disservices—they render will be influenced by the proclivities and competencies of their heads, your appointees.

This memorandum identifies some features of particular cabinet posts which may be converted into assets or liabilities for you, by the personal qualities of the department head concerned.

I have not tried to cover all departments. Omissions can be dealt with later, if and as you wish.

State and Defense

Everybody who is knowledgeable on these two departments and on NSC can tell you that the personalities and interests of your appointees will make a profound difference to the workings of the government in the national security sphere. Undoubtedly you will be urged to think through work relationships, and operating methods, and desired organization, in advance of choosing your two secretaries.

In general, this is always good advice.

In these two cases, though, it seems wholly irrelevant. Given the limited number of men you have to choose among and given the urgency of early choice, you simply cannot take the time to survey organizations or to plumb all quirks of personality and interest in your appointees.

Pick your men quickly on the grounds that are immediately relevant. Then let us "experts" worry about staff arrangements you may need to compensate for qualities or interests they may lack.

Treasury

This is a post of massive institutional power. The bread-and-butter work of the department includes tax administration, customs collection, currency control, debt and trust-fund management, public borrowing, and a variety of semisupervisory relationships with leading agencies.

Treasury is the government's financial agent. Traditionally it is, as well, the financial community's "spokesman" in the cabinet. Its work holds cardinal interest also for tax lawyers and their clients. It is on a special footing with congressional committees as a source of tax proposals. It is viewed abroad as though it were a full-fledged finance ministry. It has a statutory claim to guide our people at the World Bank and the [International] Monetary Fund. It has a statutory link to the Export-Import Bank. Its cooperation is important to the Federal Reserve Board. And by custom, though not law, Treasury has a permanent seat on the National Security Council.

Under contemporary conditions at home and abroad, the Treasury thus occupies a central, strategic place in any administration. It has one foot firmly planted in domestic economics, the other in foreign relations. Of all the civilian departments it is best equipped to claim and play a major role in both these spheres of policy at once. Secretary [George] Humphrey and Secretary [Robert] Anderson were not just men of personal force and charm with excellent connections. They were also men operating from an institutional base, of statutory mandates and of technical staffs, which validated and supported their involvement in everybody else's business. Your secretary of the Treasury will operate from the same base.

There is much to be said for bowing to tradition and drawing your secretary out of the financial community. He will have to deal with that community continuously in any case, debt management being what it is these days. His daily duties cannot help but make him sensitive to the concerns of bankers and investors, their colleagues overseas, and their friends on the Hill. He will end as a "spokesman" for them. He might as well begin as an effective spokesman to them. You can gain some advantage from that.

But you scarcely stand to gain unless the man is widely known and much respected in those circles. Truman got no mileage out of [John] Snyder's reputation, such as it was. In terms of reputation and ability you need a Humphrey not a Snyder. But the disadvantages would far outweigh the gains if he should be a man remotely as conservative or isolationist as Humphrey.

Your chance for net advantage seems to lie in a man who both fits the tradition and transcends it: a [Robert] Lovett, a [John] McCloy, a [Douglas] Dillon; a "Wall Street internationalist," sophisticated in foreign affairs and prepared for "positive government." Since Treasury is actually a major foreign policy post, you would be advantaged further if your man had had a previous experience in State. Since Treasury also is a key domestic policy post, you would want him sympathetic with your general feel for the domestic order of priorities. Considering the nature of his job, your secretary of the Treasury, no matter who he is, inevitably will tend to be on the "conservative" side of numerous specific policy disputes in your administration. But provided he is not "agin" your own sense of direction, you have nothing to fear from that.

If you follow these specifications, you are likely to end with a registered Republican. Assuming he were qualified in other respects, this could give you still another advantage: the symbolisms of "bipartisanship" and "fiscal responsibility" rolled into one. But you do not want to pay a costly price for this, once you have taken office. You and your secretary of state and other close associates ought to be confident that he would wear well as a working colleague before you take him into your official family. Among Republicans, [Henry] Stimsons and [Robert] Lovetts are not met with every day; and superficial resemblances can be deceiving. It would be better to forgo the symbolism and to settle for a Democratic known quantity, than to risk a Martin Durkin [Eisenhower's first secretary of labor] case in Treasury.

Justice

Depending on his personal qualities, the attorney general can be an enormous asset to the President, or a passive drag, or a decided liability. But the full utility of Justice as a presidential asset has not often been perceived by sitting Presidents. Truman never understood the value he could get, so never got it. Instead, he saddled himself with some extraordinary liabilities. Roosevelt did better, but only [Robert] Jackson gave him something like a full return on his investment in the Justice job. Eisenhower has avoided the worst pitfalls, but has scarcely had a Jackson. Nobody since Coolidge has had a Harlan Stone, who may have been the best attorney general in this century. And Coolidge's good fortune was the product of necessity in Harding's aftermath.

You stand to gain some seven things from your attorney general:

First is a set of high-powered, hard-driving, scrupulous, intelligent assistants overseeing the department's work in civil rights, immigration, antitrust, tax prosecutions, claims.

Second is a personnel policy which draws in first-rate talent from the best law schools and law firms, to freshen and enliven the divisions (and the solicitor general's office).

Third is a hand-hold on a patronage potential of the department itself—especially U.S. attorneys' offices—and on the flow of senatorial patronage: the judgeships.

Fourth is a watching brief (it scarcely can be more in present circumstances) on the Federal Bureau of Investigation.

Fifth is a watching brief on standards of good conduct in the regulatory and procurement agencies which lie outside of Justice but not beyond the reach of its investigators (and prosecutors). A first line of defense against corruption is a widespread sense of vigilance and inquiry at Justice. A second line of defense is a constant check upon the quality of regulatory appointments. This too an attorney general can provide.

Sixth is effective contact with and counsel to the judiciary committees, in particular, and to congressional sources generally, as chief law officer of the government, and as a representative of your administration.

Seventh is informal but effective contact with the chief justice and with key federal judges on matters of judicial administration, and otherwise.

You are not guaranteed these gains by the mere presence of a man in the attorney general's chair. The sort of man most likely to produce them for you is a commanding figure at the bar, or an outstanding dean at a great law school. The man needs toughness and intelligence. He needs administrative capabilities beyond the ordinary among lawyers. He also need be "learned in the law" and feel the whole tradition in his bones.

The men least likely to perform in your interest are sadly exemplified by Truman's attorneys general. Regarding one of them, [J. Howard] McGrath, it should be said that his "sins" were more of omission than commission. Apparently, he thought the way to reach the supreme bench was to sit quietly at Justice and avoid upsetting things. He sat until the place collapsed around him.

All attorneys general dream about the Court. You would be well advised to make sure that your man, whoever he may be, sees Justice as a testing ground and not a waiting room.

Labor

Traditionally, the secretary of labor has been viewed as "labor's voice in the cabinet," drawn either from among trade union presidents or from among politicians who could claim strong union backing. FDR departed from this tradition with Miss [Frances] Perkins. Eisenhower has departed from it with [James] Mitchell. Miss Perkins's experience is hardly relevant today, but Mitchell's is very apt. It suggests strongly that you would have much to gain from following this Eisenhower precedent.

The big thing wrong with "labor's voice" is that the unions want to deal with the President's voice when anything important is at stake for them. And managements will not take seriously any voice that they conceive is confined to a union party line. And

Congress has refused to let the labor secretary dominate conciliation services, so long as he appears to represent labor's side.

The labor secretary can be useful to you only if he can serve as a chief adviser and buffer on industrial relations. His departmental management is trifling. Miss Perkins's role as a welfare adviser was rendered wholly out of date by HEW [Department of Health, Education, and Welfare]. But the industrial relations role is barred to any man identified as merely "labor's voice."

Mitchell has been virtually in charge of FMCS [Federal Mediation and Conciliation Service]; he has been Eisenhower's deputy in dealings with NLRB [National Labor Relations Board]. He has played the role of White House mediator and adviser once assumed by [John] Steelman [for Truman], who was literally at the White House. Unions, managements, and Congress have accepted Mitchell in these roles as they rarely were willing to accept his predecessors. It has been Eisenhower's gain.

In your administration, the unions may not acquiesce as readily in a de facto "secretary for industrial relations" short of you. But the effort is worth making. And the unions lose nothing substantial if you make it. The time has long since passed when they need a "voice" in the cabinet to assure themselves a hearing in the conduct of government.

Symbolically, of course, your happiest solution might well be the one advanced for Treasury: a man who both fits the tradition and transcends it; a man out of the unions with such qualities and reputation that all sides will accept him as a "secretary for industrial relations." So far as I know there is only one such man: Arthur Goldberg. And even though he, clearly, is among the ablest men in public life, it may be questionable whether his former employers could accustom themselves quickly to the view that he was your counsel, not theirs.

Failing a Goldberg, the next best bet would seem to be a man who is at once leading arbitrator-mediator and *persona grata* in the trade union community. . . .

Commerce

Once again there is an old tradition. In this instance it is not an easy one to break, and hardly worth breaking: Commerce is the "voice of business" in the cabinet. But as with Treasury there is no law that says the secretary's spokesmanship has to be all one way.

Conceivably a businessman could be found who was at once successful in his private undertakings and of much your mind in his own public policy outlook. If he were also sharp and energetic, he might be effective as a spokesman for you; conceivably, a man of this sort even might give bite and point to departmental management, something Commerce has not felt for years. The formula, again, is to meet the tradition and transcend it. This will take some doing. . . .

Memo 4
White House Titles

For: Theodore Sorensen
December 3, 1960

Regarding that piece of paper you showed me Tuesday, if the senator [Kennedy] is thinking of an early public announcement, I suggest:

(1) Call [Lawrence] O'Brien "secretary to the President," or alternatively, "special assistant to the President." If you wish to have only one "secretary," use the other title, but there is no absolute reason why the President should have but one. FDR had three, and only gradually were these distinguished by the added (and initially unofficial) designations: "press," "appointments," etc.

(2) Call the "Gordon Gray counterpart" and the "military-intelligence liaison" aide "special assistants to the President," or alternatively, "special consultants," which I would like better since it sounds less permanent.

(3) Call [Richard E.] Neustadt (if announced with the rest) a "special consultant to the President." "Consultant" leaves everything open, including the advisory committee question. And this is a well-established White House title for part-timers with special advisory jobs.

Do not include specific assignments in the titles of "special assistants" or "consultants." Do not, for example, give O'Brien a title like "special assistant for personnel and congressional liaison," or the

NSC man a title like "special assistant for national security affairs," or me a title like "special consultant for government organization."

White House titles should be unspecific. Assignments to individuals can be indicated without being frozen into their titles. This makes it easier to shift their assignments (or men) later and prevents automatic formation of a clientele with which the man is openly identified (especially important to avoid in O'Brien's case).

Incidentally, in the case of the NSC counterpart, even if his job is to be shifted later from the White House staff to the executive secretaryship, he needs to start off with a White House title and to hold both titles in tandem, for a while, in order publicly to upgrade the executive secretary's job, which has been downgraded by years of identification with the personality of Jimmy Lay.

Memo 5
A White House Aide for Personnel and Congressional Liaison

For: President-Elect John F. Kennedy
December 7, 1960

Two weeks ago, at Palm Beach, I gained the impression that you had in mind a continuing job on the White House staff, to be built around the recurrent chores of screening and selecting personnel for presidential appointments. I understood that the man who did this after January 20 also would keep watch on departmental personnel actions, keep an eye on political organization in the states, and give you general utility assistance with congressional relations. I gathered that Larry O'Brien was the man you had in mind.

This strikes me as a fine combination of functions and a nice fit of man to job. If it still strikes you that way and still represents your intentions, I recommend the following:

(1) Take O'Brien out of his present context fast. Every day that he remains "out front" in personnel selection, with his campaign title, his National Committee locals, and his newspaper billing as the Party's "man to see" makes it harder for him to assume the White House work you have in mind and carry it [out] effectively.

However, if he were to come into your White House circle without another front-man in his place, the heat, the finger-pointing, and the blame would move with him right to your doorstep and to you. Much of this may now be inescapable, but much can still be ducked if someone else, outside the circle, becomes buffer and heat-taker in his stead.

Accordingly, I urge two things:

First: Have [Senator] Jackson announce a successor to O'Brien in O'Brien's present job as "director of organization." What counts is not the title but the notion of successor for the job that he has done. The man who is so labeled would have to look like the successor, the more so since he would not really be one, save in part.

Jackson should also announce that this step had been taken, with your approval, because you had other work in mind for O'Brien.

Second: When the press asks, you could say that you intend to keep O'Brien with you and to have him continue after January 20 as a "special assistant to the President" (your wording for [Kenneth] O'Donnell, at the postelection press conference could serve again), and that you had a lot of work in mind for him, period.

When it comes to permanent titles, you may wish to use the old and honorable "secretary to the President" for O'Donnell, or O'Brien, or both. But "special assistant" suffices for now and could suffice permanently if you wished. The one thing I would not do in O'Brien's case—or any other, for that matter—is follow Eisenhower's precedent of including job descriptions in White House titles. Except for the press secretary (where the descriptive word is an unshakable tradition) the blander and more generalized these titles, the better and more flexible for you. Washingtonians learn fast enough who does what; there is no need to freeze assignments by the titles given staff men. In O'Brien's case, particularly, much could be lost by advertising him as the personnel man or the congressional liaison.

(2) Give O'Brien a buffer on the civil service side as well as on the National Committee side. For everybody's sake—especially your own—it is important to avoid a widespread impression that your political personnel adviser was also the man from whom you took advice on career civil service matters. To a considerable extent he should be; but he should not seem to be. Therefore, before

O'Brien's bundle of White House assignments gets identified around town, I urge again (as in my memo of October 30) that you publicly announce your intention to redesignate Roger Jones as chairman of the Civil Service Commission, for the time being, and that you intend to use him as a general-purpose adviser on career personnel matters. . . .

(3) Go slow on staffing up congressional liaison. With O'Brien retrieved from the [Democratic National] Committee, I would urge caution on his part, and yours, in building up a staff of liaison assistants. He will need help, no doubt, but how much help, how well identified, with what assignments and relationships are questions to be weighed with care. An overorganized White House liaison operation—like the one Eisenhower built in his first term—tends to turn presidential staffers into chore-boys for congressmen and bureaucrats alike. From this the President has more to risk than to gain, in my opinion.

Once you give the signal on O'Brien, I will offer what I can by way of help in thinking through "next steps" on staffing for liaison.

(4) In spelling out O'Brien's job, leave room for it to grow. The assignments you have had in mind for him might grow in two spheres, over time:

First is the sphere of trading-stock with congressmen in terms of "pork," not patronage. In recent decades, so far as I know, there has never been a systematic, sustained effort to make departmental budgets, and procurements, and contracts regularly serve the President's own purposes with Congress. The efforts made from time to time have been spotty, often ineffectual. A systematic effort would be hard to organize, harder to sustain, perhaps impossible, but well worth exploration.

Second is the sphere of presidential party organization, reaching out and down to key localities. Again, it would be worthwhile to explore what could be done, and how, by far more systematic effort than has been applied in the recent past.

Memo 6
The National Security Council: First Steps

For: President-Elect John F. Kennedy
December 8, 1960

You will shortly receive from Senator Jackson a prepublication version of his subcommittee's staff report on NSC. As a subcommittee consultant, I have had a hand in that report and subscribe to its sentiments. But since it is intended as a public document, it ducks the concrete question: What are you to do about the NSC between now and January 20? This memorandum is addressed to that question.

An NSC Assistant

Very soon after you announce your cabinet selections of State, Defense, and Treasury I urge you to designate a "special assistant" (or "consultant") who would work in the national security field, and have [Clark] Clifford introduce him to the Eisenhower administration as the *pro tem* counterpart for all the following:

Special Assistant to the President for National Security Affairs (Gordon Gray)
Special Assistant to the President for Security Operations Coordination (Karl Harr)
Special Assistant to the President for Foreign Economic Affairs (Clarence Randall)

Special Consultant to the President for Foreign Agricultural Affairs (Clarence Francis)
Executive Secretary of the National Security Council (James Lay)
Executive Officer of the Operations Coordinating Board (Bromley Smith).

Designation now as your "assistant," along with such broad "counterparting," would establish this man's role in your entourage, without committing him or you, prematurely, to particular titles and organizational announcements. The role is a personal assistantship to you, involving staff work on foreign-military policy matters, police work on interdepartmental relations, and management of NSC machinery (see below).

The role should be created and the man should be identified before your cabinet designees develop fixed ideas about their roles. Otherwise, your man would be at a perpetual disadvantage in his dealing with them. But you will be advantaged if you indicate the role and name the man without deciding organizational details for the time being.

Once you name him, he and I can go over the tentative arrangements sketched below and give you firm proposals for decisions on detail as need arises in the coming weeks. Since the evolving roles of [Theodore] Sorensen and [David] Bell will be affected by the evolution of this NSC assistant's job, it would be well for their sakes, let alone your own, if you made these decisions no sooner than you had to.

The sort of man you need to fill the role is well exemplified by Robert Tufts, or by Paul Nitze if you do not use him elsewhere. On reflection, I incline to favor Tufts over Nitze for this particular assignment since it seems to be "anonymous," pure staff work, perhaps too confining for Nitze's personal force and public standing. But my preference is relative, subjective, and arguable. Both men would know what to do and how to do it. If you plan different uses for them both, others of their sort exist. I can give you more names if you wish.

A Tentative Plan for NSC Staffing

Although there is no need to settle all details just now, you do need to reach a tentative conclusion on the main lines of NSC organization and operation when you first take office. You need to have a sense of where you mean to go, which you can talk out with your man before you first appoint him as an interim assistant. Details can be deferred. The general outline should be clear in both your minds from the start of your relationship.

In terms of guidelines, not details on organization, I recommend the following:

(1) Combine the Gordon Gray and James Lay jobs. After Inauguration make your man executive secretary of the NSC, in place of Lay (Lay could remain as a consultant until a suitable career job were found for him). Then, by executive order, transfer to your secretary the functions of all Eisenhower's White House assistants and consultants in this sphere.

The executive secretaryship of NSC is a statutory post filled by presidential appointment without Senate confirmation; its formal status is the same, in other words, as the budget directorship. Over the years it has acquired a neutral, colorless, paper-pushing, "secretariat-ish" character, by virtue of Lay's own concepts and personality. But the statute does not make it so, and there is nothing to prevent you from using it (in the fashion originally intended) as the place for your own staff man on national security affairs.

Since Lay has downgraded the job in bureaucratic eyes, his successor should continue as a "special assistant to the President," holding both titles until his own performance upgraded the statutory one to the point where the other could quietly be dropped.

You stand to gain two things by moving in this direction: First, you avoid encumbering the White House, your personal office, with a functionally specialized assistant who will need substantial staff of his own, Second, you avoid the layering of staffs that has been characteristic in Eisenhower's time. The NSC executive secretary (new style) would be as much your man as if he were in the White House, but since he holds the statutory title he could build an NSC staff in the Executive Office and manage it directly, without anyone between him and the underlying organization. His position would be comparable to David Bell's: The President's man heading an Executive Office agency.

Your man stands to gain something also. Without ceasing to be your confidential assistant, he gains status as an official one step outside the "palace," with a certain dignity in his own right. Like the budget director, he would be something more than just another "palace guardsman" whose status depended wholly on the intimacy of his relationship with you.

(2) Combine the ongoing personnel and functions of the Council on Economic Foreign Policy, the Operations Coordination Board, and the NSC secretariat into a single NSC staff under the direction of the executive secretary. This requires only an executive order. Once formally combined, that miscellany of staffs and interagency committees could be slimmed down, reoriented (and in part repopulated) into a tight group of very able general utility assistants to your assistant. There are approximately seventy-four people now employed by these various entities. It is unlikely that a Nitze or a Tufts would need a staff of that size, once he had pruned, transplanted, and replaced existing personnel.

(3) Treat your NSC assistant from the outset as a full-fledged member of your staff circle, a collaborator with the Sorensens and Bells as well as an assistant to you. It is vital that your NSC man should work closely and collegially with the special counsel, the budget director (and, in due course, with your economic and science advisers). The fact that he is "specializing" in national security policy should not obscure their need to know a lot about his undertakings or his need to know a lot about theirs. (In many ways they all have to be specialists in national security policy; it is the most important segment of governmental policy.) Moreover, his relationship to the NSC should not restrict your use of him for ad hoc staff assistance of the sort you claim from others. He should stand ready, when need be, to take his turn at trouble-shooting, fire-fighting, without undue concern about the confines of his "specialty."

A Tentative Approach to NSC Operations

Agreement with your NSC assistant on the main lines of future organization should be buttressed by agreement on the main lines of council operations after January 20. Before you choose your man you need to make a general judgment on this score, which you can then talk out with him. In terms of operations, my recommendations are as follows:

(1) The council is an advisory body to you. It should meet on your call when you want advice on something, and not otherwise. If members want a meeting they can urge you to call it, asking through your NSC assistant, or directly. If you want a meeting for a special purpose involving less than the full membership, do not ask the others to attend. When the press asks why you are not "using NSC," you can hide behind the fiction of a "subcommittee," if you wish, or stand upon your rights to seek advice in any way you choose.

NSC members, after all, also are department heads and cabinet officers. They wear three hats as advisers to you, and you will no doubt want them to advise you in different ways under different hats at different times. Nothing requires you to make them wear their NSC hat each time they come in. Nothing prevents you from saying that they wore it if it suits your convenience to say so.

(2) Whenever you meet with two or more NSC members (whether the meeting were identified with NSC or not) it would be well if your own NSC assistant sat in as an observer, to keep the continuity (except when you don't want him there for reasons of your own).

(3) When you meet with the full council (Vice President, State, Defense, OCDM [Office of Civilian Defense Mobilization], JCS [Joint Chiefs of Staff] as observers, and Treasury by custom though not statute), it would be well if Sorensen and Bell were present as observers also.

(4) Apart from your staff, keep a tight rein on the members' right to bring their own staffs into meetings. These should be sessions of principals, not aides, and kept as small as possible. In Robert Lovett's phrase: "Any principal who has not done his homework should receive the grade of 'D'" from you.

(5) Meetings of the council (or a "subcommittee" thereof) should be regarded as vehicles for sharpening differences of view on major policy departures or on new courses of action advocated by

the secretary of state, or by the secretary of defense, or tossed in by you as a trial balloon. The agenda should be in your hands (with help from your NSC assistant), and you should make it clear that what you want on agenda items is an airing of divergent views, not an effort at centered agreement. Minor issues and conversations about "general" goals should be kept off your agenda; so should major issues not yet ripe for sharp, informed discussions.

(6) If NSC is to operate along the foregoing lines, some official must be charged with continuing responsibility for raising the hard, difficult policy departures and new courses with which it would be concerned. Depending on the skills and interests of your appointees, this official should be either your secretary of state (backed by his director for policy planning) or your NSC assistant if—and only if—State cannot be relied on for continuing initiative. Either way, you should remain free to seize the initiative yourself, whenever and as often as you choose. Meetings will gain vitality from your activity.

(7) In addition to NSC meetings, there probably will be recurrent need for preliminary or supplemental meetings where the agencies concerned are represented not by principals but by high-caliber subordinates. For this purpose it may be desirable to continue something like (though far less formal than) the planning board. But for many, if not most purposes, interdepartmental meetings at second level should be tailored for the particular problem involved. Ad hoc working groups, built around some member of the NSC staff (or a departmental staff), would be the preferred vehicles for preliminary "planning" and for "operations coordination."

(8) Assuming that you do not appoint a director of OCDM, and let it continue for the time being with a careerist as "acting director," he should be asked, politely, to stay away from NSC meetings. On the other hand, assuming that your chairman of the Council of Economic Advisers is broad-gauged enough to make CEA a full-fledged economic and resources program staff, he might be asked to sit on NSC in OCDM's place. The National Security Act intended that one member regularly bring to bear

perspective on the domestic economy and domestic resources. CEA could be a far more serviceable source than OCDM of "domestic" perspective appropriate to the 1960s.

Concluding Note

Once these first steps are taken and a man appointed, there will be next steps to plan, in terms of organizational details, of precedents to set at a first NSC meeting, and of still other precedents to set in NSC's relationships with budget preparations. I will try to deal with these in later memoranda.

Memo 7
Shutting Down Eisenhower's "Cabinet System"

For: President-Elect John F. Kennedy
December 20, 1960

At the end of this month I will send you a memorandum of recommendations on procedures for your cabinet meetings, and on the matter of setting precedents at the first meeting.

Meanwhile, let me call to your attention that Eisenhower's formal cabinet "system" includes not only a White House "secretary to the cabinet" but "cabinet assistants" at the secretary's level in each department. These assistants are supposed to recommend agenda items to the cabinet secretary, brief their principals before each cabinet meeting, and be briefed themselves, by White House staff, on what transpired when the cabinet met. A lot of paper passes to and fro between them and the cabinet secretary.

Cabinet assistantships are part-time jobs in most departments, held by personal assistants to department heads. As your cabinet officers begin to staff up, they are likely to be told of these jobs and to assign their own aides to them. Once a newcomer is designated "cabinet assistant," he is likely to find out what his predecessor did—and do likewise. Before long, vested interests in the present cabinet system would spring up in each of your departments. This ought to be avoided.

Therefore, I urge you to pass the word to your department heads that you intend to examine Eisenhower's cabinet procedures before anything carries over into the new administration; and that until you have done so they should hold off on the cabinet assistantships they will find in their departments.

Memo 8
Appointing Fred Dutton "Staff Secretary" Instead of "Cabinet Secretary"

For: President-Elect John F. Kennedy
December 23, 1960

On Thursday night you mentioned that you had decided to bring Fred Dutton on the White House staff, and you indicated roughly what you had in mind for him to do.

With this I have no quarrel, but I do quarrel with the title you mentioned for him: "secretary to the cabinet." This is an Eisenhower title, redolent of Ike's faith in "system" and "teamwork," and, as presently used, it connotes elaborate, formalized procedures for cabinet meetings which you almost certainly will want to scrap.

If you appoint a "secretary to the cabinet," the bureaucracy will assume that you, like Ike, intend to try to use the cabinet, per se, as a major forum for policy-making. So far as I know, you have nothing of the sort in mind. Also, it will be assumed that you intend to keep Ike's elaborate system of agendas and cabinet "papers." I doubt that you will want to be one-half as formal. Finally, it will be assumed that somehow you are reverting to the Eisenhower "staff system." The "secretary to the cabinet" has been one of the most publicized (though least successful) features of that system.

I wouldn't touch this title with a ten-foot pole.

Instead, I suggest that you give Dutton the title—and the job—of "staff secretary to the President." This is the title [Andrew]

Goodpaster holds for the publicized part of his job (the other part of Goodpaster's job, military and intelligence liaison, is separate from his work as staff secretary and naturally would not be assumed by Dutton). When you appoint Dutton to this post, your press statement could state that you intend to merge with the staff secretaryship such work of the existing cabinet secretariat as you decide to continue. This merger makes sense, anyway, quite apart from Dutton.

[Clark] Clifford then could introduce Dutton at the White House as your counterpart for Goodpaster (in the public part of his job) and for the cabinet secretary, also. This would make the point with the bureaucracy that you were shifting emphasis and not reverting toward Eisenhower's "system."

The job of staff secretary was originally thought up by Don Price and recommended in the first Hoover Commission reports. As originally visualized, the staff secretary was to be the "housekeeper" and "timekeeper" of White House staff work. On the President's behalf he was to keep track of documents requiring action, of assignments requiring execution, of decisions reached in cabinet meetings and elsewhere. The staff secretary was to be a facilitator of the work of everybody else, not a competitor but a watcher of everybody's doings, keeping lines straight, untangling snarls, watching deadlines, checking on performance.

As such the staff secretary was to be associated very closely with the White House executive clerk, Bill Hopkins, and was to act for the President as supervisor of the clerk and of White House administrative services.

Truman never picked up this Hoover Commission recommendation, but Eisenhower did, and this is an Eisenhower innovation which has proved useful.

With Hopkins as a most reliable assistant, Eisenhower's staff secretary has not been overly burdened by the paper-processing and administrative service aspects of his job. Dutton would not be overly burdened either. He could easily take on whatever agenda-making and decision-recording you wish for cabinet meetings. He also could have time to serve as one of your "handholders" for heads of agencies with operating inquiries and troubles which appear too petty (or too premature) to bring to you. Finally, he could serve, when you want him to, on spot assignments like speech writing, in association with other members of your staff.

This bundle of duties seems reasonable and practicable to me—and the title of "staff secretary" fits them better than any other available to you. It is bland enough so that you could use Dutton flexibly and change his duties as your future needs suggest. But the title carries with it enough fixed assignments—in terms of paper-processing, assignment-watching, deadline-checking—to give him useful work to do each day, regardless of your other needs for him.

Dutton's role will evolve and change, no doubt, as your needs and his talents and interstaff relationships develop. Meanwhile, with the title "staff secretary" he has a useful anchor, and you avoid the undesirable "public relations" consequences of reviving the "cabinet secretary" title.

One thing more: The staff secretary's job, as described above, will have to be done as a service job not only for you but for the other major members of your staff: [Kenneth] O'Donnell, [Lawrence] O'Brien, and [Theodore] Sorensen. Dutton needs to be a facilitator, helper-outer, informant, and friend of all. Otherwise, he gets in everybody's way.

Memo 9
Location of Disarmament Agency

For: Dean Rusk
January 2, 1961

Ten days ago, at Palm Beach, President-elect Kennedy asked me to give you a memorandum making the following points:

(1) He has a "superficial preference" for locating the work of policy development and attendant research on "disarmament" or "arms control" in the Executive Office of the President, rather than in the Department of State.

(2) He wants you to review the pros and cons of a disarmament agency in the Executive Office. He asked me to look into these and state them for your consideration. This is done below.

(3) Once you have had opportunity to review these pros and cons, he wants you to give him your conclusions and advice on whether he should hold or change his "superficial preference."

I have held off writing you until I could satisfy myself on the character of the problem and the nature of the issues as they look at the start of a Kennedy administration (a rather different look than they have worn before). This memorandum takes account of arguments made last spring, summer, and fall; it also takes account of pending recommendations by the so-called Sharon task force in this field. But I have not tried to reproduce the views of others in their terms. The following statement of pros and cons provides you merely my best current view of what the issues are, put in my terms, as a starting point for your discussion with the President-elect.

The Assumed Alternatives

During the past year, arguments over organizational location of a central "disarmament staff" (under whatever title) have often been confused by incommensurate conceptions of the need it was supposed to meet, the job it was to do. For the sake of clarity, let me state that I assume this staff would have the following characteristics, regardless of location:

(1) Its major purpose would be to initiate policy proposals, in the sense of determinate courses of action (negotiated or unilateral) and to secure criticism of, consideration for, and decision on its initiatives by the responsible officials concerned, up to and including the President. The purpose, in short, is "policy planning" conceived concretely, not in "aspiration" terms, and conceived as thinking problems through to a conclusion, not just registering views expressed by others.

(2) Given this purpose, the staff would not be a study-group in the usual sense of "research institute," but it would be, emphatically, a formulator, designer, and consumer of studies. Its work would begin with question-asking; the quality of its policy proposals would depend on the quality of its questioning and on the competence with which it sought and appraised answers. Accordingly, technical competence "across-the-board"—military, scientific, economic, diplomatic—would have to be built into the staff itself. This does not mean a "house technician" in every narrow specialty. But it does mean capability, within the staff, to talk the language, see the perspectives, and review the propositions of the major professional and technical groups touched by the issues of arms control.

(3) This staff would need freedom to tap research facilities of other government agencies and private sources of research as well. It might also need "an IDA [Institute of Defense Analyses] of its own."

(4) Research facilities aside, a central staff with appropriate built-in competence might number up to 100 professionals, many of them in supergrades. A staff on this scale would increase, not diminish, the need for first-rate staffs elsewhere in government. Regardless of the central staff's location, it could not do its job in a vacuum. It would need counsel and ideas from staffs associated with the work (and the perspectives) of the operating agencies: State itself, Defense, AEC [Atomic Energy Commission], and others. Its policy proposals, when developed, would deserve hard thought and well-informed reactions from responsible officials in those agencies. Thus, the stronger the central staff, the greater the need for strengthened staff work elsewhere, especially at topmost levels in Defense and State.

Given the foregoing assumptions about the nature of the central staff, one additional assumption is in order: If this staff were located "in the State Department," it would have to be an "ICA [International Cooperation Administration] equivalent," an autonomous unit with its own budget and personnel and its own statutory underpinning. The restrictions of "Wristonization" and of departmental budgeting make this appear the only practicable basis on which such a staff could be built "inside" State. Accordingly, the issue of location boils down to such ICA-type status, or alternatively, to status of the Budget Bureau sort in the Executive Office of the President.

The case for each of these alternatives is made below.

The Case for Executive Office Location

(1) Status. There is need to demonstrate abroad, at home, and inside government that issues of disarmament are taken very seriously, and that policy development will be pursued with vigor by the President himself. A staff attached to his own office makes the point symbolically and practically—as nothing else can do—especially in light of recent history where [Harold] Stassen's operation from the White House was more vigorous than anything seen since.

(2) Proximity. A staff within the presidential office has a claim upon the President's attention, and a freedom to invoke that claim far greater than the claims or freedoms of subordinate units in cabinet departments.

(3) Perspective. The policy problems of arms control are as encompassing as are the duties of a President. By the same token, these problems transcend departmental jurisdiction and concerns. No department's duties furnish a perspective broad enough to match the sweep of problems. State's preoccupation with foreign relations produces a "parochial" perspective; so does the Pentagon's preoccupation with defense. All the "parochialisms" bear on policy; none suffices as a base for policy. Only the President's perspective does that. Accordingly, his office is the proper source of policy initiatives.

(4) Pentagon Relations. The Pentagon's concerns may be "parochial" but have enormous relevance for policy-making in the disarmament field. Granting other aspects, arms control contributes to defense policy; increasingly, it is recognized—and justified—as such. It also limits defense policy; negotiating positions on arms control—to say nothing of agreements—limit the Pentagon's freedom of action within its own sphere of responsibility. (The same thing can be said of AEC.) At the same time the Pentagon has technical resources, in the uniformed services and in contract facilities, which are indispensable for any set of planners who would come to grips with disarmament policy. Support from some or all of the key power centers in Defense is thus critically important for a disarmament staff.

There is reason to believe that an Executive Office staff would find it easier to gain and hold this critical support than would a staff identified with State. The State Department generally, and "diplomats" in particular, are relatively suspect at the Pentagon. This mistrust is the product partly of history, partly of differences in duty and perspective. It is not easy for responsible officers in many parts of the Pentagon to let others impose limits on the exercise of their responsibilities, especially when the others bear the label "diplomat."

Thus, State Department leadership in policy development for arms control would bear a burden of suspicion which the Pentagon, presumably, would not load on a presidential agency, at least not to the same extent. The difference has political importance for a President.

(5) Interstaff Relations. As a part of the Executive Office, the disarmament staff could look forward to close, collegial relationships with neighboring staff units. In the Kennedy administration these relationships promise to be productive. The Budget Bureau is to be revitalized; the Council of Economic Advisers is to build staff capabilities for program review and development in every major sphere of economic and social policy; the science adviser's office and the Science Advisory Committee are to take permanent form as a key staff element, providing comparable capabilities in scientific and technological spheres. The NSC's machinery is to be refashioned into a staff unit with generalist skills for program review, trouble-shooting, follow-up. These, at least, are current intentions.

In such an environment the disarmament staff should flourish, drawing strength, advice, ideas, from these associated staffs and making its own contributions to them in return. It is unlikely that a staff outside the Executive Office "family" could sustain a fully comparable relationship.

The Case for ICA-Type Location in State

(1) Precedent-Setting. What is true of disarmament policy is true, in some degree, of all foreign policy (and indeed of most domestic policy): everything transcends accustomed jurisdictions and perspectives of departments; every problem is "interdepartmental;" every issue should be set in "presidential perspective." If one followed to their logical conclusion the "status" and "perspective" arguments above, the Executive Office of the President would soon take over policy development in every sphere (and then would need New State, as well as Old, for office space).

The problem is not to hoist policy planning out of the departments, leaving cabinet posts as hollow shells, but to raise the sights and build the capabilities of departmental staffs, so that responsible department heads can think, advise, and act in terms appropriate to modern government. There is nothing "wrong" with State's traditional primacy as foreign policy adviser to the President, except State's failure to adapt its personnel and organization as befits the modern meanings and requirements of policy.

The exception is a large one, but hopefully not permanent. Somebody has to serve as a prime source of advocacy and advice;

why not the secretary of state as head of a revitalized department, appropriately staffed?

At the outset of a new administration, ready to experiment with new men and new methods, this question should be kept open. The secretary ought to have a run for the money. The quickest way to stop him short is to move the policy initiative on arms control from State—where it now rests, however poorly—and to vest the function in the Office of the President. Granting that the present disarmament staff needs redevelopment and real autonomy, these needs can be met without breaking its connection to the secretary of state.

As he begins to redevelop his own staff facilities and to reform his departmental operations, he should be spared the symbolism—and the fact—of "downgrading" his status with respect to a key element in foreign policy.

(2) New Atmosphere. In the atmosphere of Eisenhower's later years, the arguments of "status," "proximity," "perspective," and "Pentagon relations," sketched above, are more persuasive than they would appear to be in the new atmosphere of Mr. Kennedy's administration. A new disarmament staff headed by John McCloy has status, access to the President, and prospects for initial favor at the Pentagon, no matter what its placement in the governmental structure. With Paul Nitze at Defense and with a man of comparable stature in State's policy planning staff, McCloy would be well buttressed on two sides. A first-rate AEC man would be still another asset. When those who ultimately must decide upon McCloy's proposals are [Dean] Rusk, [Robert] McNamara, and, above all, [President] Kennedy, the contrast with the recent past grows sharp indeed. The arguments for an Executive Office location are diminished accordingly.

They are diminished further when one contemplates what [McGeorge] Bundy and an able science adviser could accomplish from their vantage points. The presidential staff will be equipped to check, advise, warn, needle, follow up, and keep an active President abreast of what is going on in the departments. Staff work on disarmament would scarcely go unnoticed or unwatched because it was proceeding in the State Department and not in the Executive Office.

(3) Inter-State Relations. It is often assumed that because a staff is in the Executive Office its initiatives are more likely than those of others to be carried to the President and to produce decisions. But organizational placement is of limited importance in deciding what the President decides. By and large, a President decides what he has to, when he has to. It is more advantageous for a planning staff to be associated with decision-forcing processes than to have a formal status in the presidential office. A President is busy. Formal status does not open his door often. The men who will go through that door repeatedly are those with questions he must answer by a given time. Decision-forcing processes involve recurrent deadlines which a President cannot ignore.

In the field of arms control policy, the principal decision-forcers seem to be negotiations and diplomatic developments. Deadlines are made by the dates when new instructions must reach missions abroad. Policy, in action terms, is decided in the process of confronting these particulars. A disarmament staff is more likely to influence policy if it sees the President whenever he has these things to decide than if it waits for him to find free time.

When negotiatory deadlines are involved, it is the secretary of state who has first claim on presidential time. Association with the secretary thus gives a *disarmament* staff hand-holds to the President's attention.

The budget process offers comparable hand-holds. This is the usual resort for staffs in the Executive Office; those in a position to use it effectively develop close relations with the President. But from the standpoint of a disarmament staff, budgetary issues do not seem a satisfactory substitute for negotiatory issues in asserting claims upon the President's attention. A connection to the secretary of state, and through him to the rest of the department, thus becomes a virtual necessity if the disarmament staff is to have timely contact, on advantageous terms, with presidential decisionmaking.

Short-Term Limitations on Both Alternatives

It will take time either to relocate the present Disarmament Administration in the Executive Office or to give it appropriate autonomy within the State Department. Either course requires legislative sanction. An ICA-type agency in State calls for statutory authority as well as funds. A comparable agency in the Executive Office could be set up by executive order, but authorizing legislation (or a reorganization plan) would be needed to put it on a solid footing. Otherwise, its existence, year by year, would be subject to the "Russell Amendment," which limits "agencies" created by executive order to one year of life unless Congress appropriates specifically for them.

Memo 10
The Science Adviser: First Steps

For: President-Elect John F. Kennedy
January 4, 1961

Since 1957 President Eisenhower has set up four pieces of advisory machinery at the presidential level in the field of science and technology. By doing so, he met a long-standing need, and much of his machinery has worked well. The more important parts of it should certainly be continued in the new administration.

However, the present science advisory organization is now located in the White House itself and is financed out of White House special projects funds. Thus, it lacks the stability of a continuing function of government. It takes a big bite annually out of the White House fund, and it keeps on the White House payroll a staff of roughly twenty, most of whom lack any intimate relation to the President's own work day by day.

It would be desirable to remove this organization one step out of your own House and locate it in the Executive Office of the President alongside the Council of Economic Advisers. This has a number of long-run advantages for the organization itself and has several short-run advantages for you—particularly the advantage of removing from your White House persons who are not engaged in your own daily work. When you appoint a new "science adviser," succeeding [George] Kistiakowski, you have an opportunity to begin the process of putting the science advisory function on a new footing in the Executive Office rather than the White House.

The way to do this is to announce that you are establishing the position of "science adviser to the President" in the Executive

Office of the President. This title has always been attached popularly to Eisenhower's assistant in the field, but actually Kistiakowski's title has been "special assistant to the President for science and technology." Your press statement could indicate that you are giving official status to the popular usage and in so doing are giving the function the continuity and status it deserves.

When you announce the science adviser, you should indicate that you intend to reestablish the present Science Advisory Committee in the Executive Office under its current title and with those of its current members whose terms have not expired. You can indicate that, through your science adviser, you are seeking the advice of the committee on suitable replacements for the six members whose terms have expired.

Your press statement should also indicate that your science adviser will head a staff office in the Executive Office which will furnish assistance both to him and to the committee in their task of giving advice to you.

Once you have established the science adviser in the Executive Office, funds for him, and for his staff, and for the Science Advisory Committee could be requested from Congress independently of White House appropriations. Once appropriations were obtained, the science adviser and his office would have a degree of continuity and independence they now lack. At the same time, you would be freed of the necessity to support them out of White House funds, and you would have reduced the number of people now carried on the White House payroll.

You will have to carry this organization out of White House special funds until appropriations are obtained. Hopefully, you can get the latter without taking a cut in the former, but this remains to be seen. Meanwhile, in announcing the creation of a science adviser in the Executive Office, care need be taken not to identify his staff office as an "office." You have authority by executive order to establish persons or committees in the Executive Office of the President, and these can have staff assistants, but you cannot create an "agency" by executive order without running into the Russell Amendment. This was intended to put an end to FDR's FEPC [Fair Employment Practices Committee]. It denies existence to any agency created by executive order unless Congress has appropriated funds specifically for it. A science adviser and his staff are not an agency, however, unless you capitalize the *O* (so I am told by the budget technicians).

The scientific community is very touchy about its status-recognition in the government. Having acquired a post in the White House, there may be concern when the post is removed one step to the Executive Office. But so long as it is clear that you mean to look to your science adviser for personal advice, this concern will fade rapidly. It may never arise at all if your initial press release makes plain that, in your mind, the change of status builds up the science advisory function and lends new recognition to science. I am preparing a suitable release. . . .

A number of people in the scientific community are becoming very jumpy about the imminent dissolution of the science adviser's staff and of the Science Advisory Committee. Since their concern arises because the science advisory function now has no permanent status, you have another argument for moving the function outside the White House so that the current situation will not occur again. But since the Kistiakowskis, the Jerome Wiesners, the [Isidore] Rabis, et al. are concerned as things now stand, it is desirable that whatever you decide to do be done quickly.

Memo 11
Coping with "Flaps" in the Early Days of the New Administration

For: Ted Sorensen, McGeorge Bundy, et al.
January 18, 1961

You have asked for my views on interim procedures to deal with "emergency situations" in the national security sphere during the next weeks.

At any time after noon on Friday, it is conceivable that the President might be faced with decisions involving the "buttons." If so, reliance will have to be placed on General [Andrew] Goodpaster and on arrangements previously in effect. However, from the outset Goodpaster should understand that he is working with and for [McGeorge] Bundy, and even in the short-run Bundy should take responsibility for widening time spans and obtaining advice outside the White House, where and as possible.

"Buttons" aside, other "emergency" situations may arise, less drastic in character, permitting more turn-around time, but calling for response on a 24-, 48-, 72-hour basis. These are the "flaps" with which this memorandum is concerned.

Such "limited emergencies" are likely to be of one of two types, or a blend of both: "operational," in the sense of something to be done; or "public relations," in the sense of something to be said. Either type is likely to present itself in one of two ways:

First, through information received in governmental channels, military, diplomatic, or intelligence;

Second, through pressure from the press for answers to questions posed by publicized events abroad or by governmental acts at home.

In the case of issues which present themselves "through channels," I suggest the following as guides for interim procedures:

(1) As heads of the chief operating agencies involved, the secretaries of state and defense will wish to assure themselves of an adequate flow of information to their own offices. (In the case of the secretary of defense this includes information flowing through military command channels.) The secretaries will wish to assure themselves, also, that each has rapid access to information available to the other.

(2) Since White House responsiveness will be increased by familiarity with relevant information, steps should be taken to ensure that appropriate members of the White House staff receive the same flow of initial information as do the secretaries. The White House, in turn, should be sure that the secretaries are seeing what the President sees.

(3) When either department spots a problem which seems to require interdepartmental consultation and presidential resolution, White House staff (in particular, Bundy) should be informed and should collaborate with the initiator in working out an ad hoc procedure for consultation and for reference to the President. The same thing can be said of issues which may be perceived most readily in CIA [Central Intelligence Agency] (or NASA [National Aeronautics and Space Administration]).

What counts here is that there be quick improvisation to bring together the responsible officials whose interests or perspectives are involved and to bring together, also, all appropriate information. The White House staff role is facilitative, but it will help if the same man acts as facilitator in every situation.

(4) The President should be informed from the outset of the issue that has arisen, of the background information that is relevant, and of the steps being taken preparatory to consultation with

him. Depending on the circumstances, the initiating secretary may want to carry the first word or may prefer to leave that to Bundy. In either event progress reports could be handled by Bundy informally.

What counts here is that the President be in on the act early from an informational standpoint and have an early chance to influence consultative arrangements if he wishes to do so.

(5) Besides reacting to initiatives from the departments, Bundy can provide a useful service if he holds a watching brief and takes initiative with the departments in suggesting matters which deserve priority attention from the secretaries. Some potential "flaps" lurk in governmental operations outside the jurisdiction of State and Defense: in NASA, for example, and in CIA. In some cases, the White House staff may be in a better position to spot these early than are State or Defense.

What counts here is that the secretary of state, particularly, be seized of issues early and that ad hoc consultative arrangements be made quickly. If the White House staff sees something that State's staff has not, Bundy should feel free to raise it.

(6) At the President's level, everything relates to everything else, and all senior members of the White House staff will have interests, perspectives, or work assignments which bear upon, or can contribute to, the resolution of "emergency" situations. This is particularly true in the case of [Ted] Sorensen.

It is no less important for Bundy to serve as a steady source of facilitation within the White House than it is for him to serve in a comparable capacity with operating agencies.

In the case of issues which present themselves primarily through press pressure, it is vital, especially in the early days, that these get treated in the same fashion as do issues arising "through channels." This means that press officers should transmit pressure up, make free use of "no comment," and not allow themselves to take on problems or to try their hand at resolution in "public relations" terms.

When an issue has a public relations aspect—as most of them will—it is important to treat this aspect in policy terms. It is also important to involve the members of the presidential staff who have continuing responsibility for policy statements. On sensitive matters every press release becomes a policy statement and should be treated as such. Accordingly, whenever public statements may figure in the outcome, Sorensen as well as Bundy should be brought into consultation at a very early stage. (Even if the outcome is to be wholly in terms of unpublicized action, Sorensen need be informed, though less currently, for the sake of policy pronouncements or actions in related spheres.)

It seems to me important that all parties deal with one another continuously, informally, and flexibly during the early weeks. These weeks could well be regarded as an educative period for them—and for the President—in terms of issues and relationships, alike. It also is an educative period for staffs, especially the staffs in the two departments, in CIA, and in the NSC complex. This is a time when an investment in personal involvement by responsible officials will pay great dividends later on.

Each secretary will need a "deputy" on the "flap" front. The deputy should be someone very close to him and someone who will play a continuing role. In the eyes of departmental staffs, important precedents will be set in the first weeks; this should be kept in mind as particular men are "deputized." Bundy will also need a "deputy" in the sense of a watch-officer. Presumably, Goodpaster is the man to take this on temporarily.

In his first two or three days on the job, the President may well be "looking for work." I have suggested to [Kenneth] O'Donnell that Mr. Kennedy announce his intention to use his first ten days as a time for study and evaluation of operating problems, particularly in the national security area. If this announcement is made, something real should happen. Any issues which have reached the point of action—or of hard discussion about preparations for action—should be taken up with him early next week.

Memo 12
Possible Remarks by the President at the Outset of the Cabinet Meeting

For: President John F. Kennedy
January 26, 1961

(Prepared by Neustadt and Fred Dutton)

(These are intended only to suggest points to be covered rather than for specific language.)

I want to take a few moments at the outset here this morning to indicate my views on the uses of the cabinet and how these meetings should operate.

The memoirs of cabinet officers are full of complaints about cabinet meetings being timewasters. Hopefully, the precedents can be improved upon.

This is not the place to try to settle concrete issues of policy. Most issues will involve less than full cabinet memberships; most need to be worked out as they arise in other kinds of meetings with the men specifically concerned.

But these meetings can most usefully serve other purposes. Formal meetings like this one will be called for several purposes:

(1) Background information on which the whole group should be briefed so that all members of the administration have a common understanding. Today's briefings are an example.

(2) Plans or ideas which all the group should know about or on which group reactions are wanted.
(3) Administrative matters of common concern to all department heads.

As an example, everyone at the table should be careful not to make public remarks about or take public stands on legislative proposals which may become part of the administration's program in advance of the President's messages. Department heads should be careful, and their staff should be equally careful. This word needs to be spread around.

Now for just a moment as to how we approach problems here. I always want your full and frank views on all issues on the agenda. I want to be sure that I get your best judgment about problems regardless of whose department they fall within.

I understand that in President Wilson's time, the secretary of war said to the secretary of the Navy, "I don't care a damn about the Navy and you don't care a damn about the Army. You run your machine and I'll run mine. . . ." That attitude may be fine back in your departments; but here in the cabinet room, I need directness and incisiveness.

In the discussions here, I am hopeful you will provide stimulating alternatives of choice, not previously agreed conclusions or merchandising with elaborate presentations. I want specific proposals for action rather than just a playback of what is wrong. For a new President, it was somewhat disturbing to read President Roosevelt's reported remark at a cabinet meeting: "I am sick and tired of being told by the cabinet, by Henry (Morgenthau), and by everybody else for the past two weeks what is the matter with the country, and nobody suggests what I should do." Let's have none of that here.

The final major point I want to make is that despite all the tugging and pulling on you by Congress, your career people, the particular groups which the various agencies serve, or anyone else, I shall need and expect your complete personal and public loyalty. And on each issue that comes before us, I shall expect you to make paramount not the viewpoint of your individual agency but the overriding national interest which the President must protect and promote.

I want to take an additional moment on several procedural matters. It is my present intention that cabinet meetings shall be held on Thursday mornings at 10 A.M. But I do not want to take your time unless there is something important for us to discuss. Meetings will consequently be held only on call. As a precaution, you should hold Thursday mornings on your schedules at least for the next several weeks. Occasionally I may have cabinet luncheons instead of formal meetings so that we can informally get together about some of our problems—and hopes.

The agenda will be determined by me. But I will appreciate individual cabinet members' regularly sending suggestions for it. I would usually like to have you raise specific problems and sharpened issues, not just general subject areas.

Whenever time permits, I would like to have brief background papers prepared on each problem coming up for discussion. That should take care of the fatty generalizations and factual details that would waste our time here. These materials will be distributed to you through my office, and I hope you will take your homework seriously.

I am hopeful we can keep these gatherings relatively small in size. We can facilitate candid discussion by that. The chairman of my Council of Economic Advisers, the director of the Bureau of the Budget, my special counsel, and my special assistant for the cabinet will attend to provide information when needed, but will not sit at the table nor participate unless called upon. Fewer of the independent agency heads will also be invited unless we are to consider a matter of special import to them.

Finally, I want to emphasize that all views and business done around this table are in confidence. No minutes will be kept, nor will there be other records except action directives which I may send from time to time.

Without further delay, let us proceed—experimenting as we go. But let us not waste time.

Part 3

Neustadt Memos from Reagan to Clinton

Memo 13
Historical Problems in Staffing the White House

For: James Baker III
December 1, 1980

Jonathan Moore has asked me, on your behalf, to think about the history of White House organization, identifying "hard nuts" your predecessors cracked teeth on. This memorandum is a quick response. Below I offer seven such things. If time and space allowed, I'd list another seven. If you want more, I'll try to oblige; however, there's a quandary: the history gets more useful the more it can be brought to bear on your specifics, but I understand how hard it is to share such things with strangers. So it has to be your nickel, as we used to say when I was young and that's what phone calls cost.

The problems identified below are more procedural than structural, more interpersonal than "institutional." This reflects the nature of the institution. Power at the White House is never the same from one year to the next, always subtly changing. Except where otherwise noted, "White House" for present purposes includes the White House staff per se along with the present NSC and Domestic Policy staffs, but not the rest of the Executive Office agencies.

Seven items follow: (1) coping with the President's own operating style, (2) compensating for mismatches in the styles of others, (3) filling jobs because they're there, (4) slashing jobs too soon, (5) forming cabinet councils, (6) linking foreign with domestic perspectives, (7) holding staff size down. By no means do these exhaust the organizational problems of your predecessors which will very likely come upon you too. Far from it. These are merely ones I've had time to consider.

1. Coping with the President's Own Operating Style

Harry Truman was instinctively a judge: bring him something to decide, and he'd usually review it in its own terms, weigh the pros and cons before him, make a quick decision, and go on to the next thing. Franklin Roosevelt, by comparison, was an intelligence operative. Bring him something to decide, and he'd often weave and bob, looking around corners for its links with other choices, wondering what he'd not been told, and probing to find out through other sources.

Truman's style produced a lot of shooting from the hip until he came to have some rather orderly procedures manned by conscientious people passing choices up to him, especially in diplomacy, limited hostilities, budgeting, legislative programming, the dominant spheres of action for his time. But nobody could make an intelligence operative out of him. One-thing-at-a-time-in-its-own-terms remained his characteristic approach. And nobody succeeded in injecting into preparatory staff work a Rooseveltian regard for the connectedness of things (or for separate checks through independent sources). Indeed, few of Truman's aides seem ever to have consciously addressed that as a problem to be solved. Rather, they lived with it and coped with consequences catch-as-catch-can. Some of his worst misadventures historically—as for instance when he seized the whole steel industry to keep a few defense production items flowing—reflect limited peripheral vision in his White House organization as well as in him.

Every administration reshapes inherited White House structure and procedure to meet the man's own preferred way of doing work. It took Truman's regime two full years to shake down in this respect (with [George] Marshall at State, [James] Webb at Budget, and [Clark] Clifford as counsel). Some have succeeded better and faster in this, notably Eisenhower after Truman, or Kennedy after Eisenhower, or Nixon's regime, for that matter, although it evidently indulged his preferences too far (as indeed did Carter's). But up to now none has succeeded equally and simultaneously in compensating for the limitations native to the man's own style.

Here's a challenge for you.

2. Compensating for Mismatches in the Styles of Others

When John F. Kennedy appointed McGeorge Bundy his assistant for national security affairs, JFK did not know he was creating the precursor of the Kissinger office under Nixon. Far from it, Kennedy was only seeking "somebody I can talk to when I don't want to bother Bob McNamara or Dean Rusk." Kennedy knew neither of those men when he appointed them, but he expected both to be what McNamara turned out to be, a vigorous, engaging analyst and advocate, diplomacy matching defense. Departmental duties would compete for their attention, and he couldn't always reach them at a moment's notice. So Bundy would be constantly at hand to pass the word, a living link among the three of them.

But Rusk turned out to be "unaccountably" reticent. Often he was absent from the crucial meeting, or, if there, he often kept his mouth shut, or his comments lacked directness, or he dropped the argument. McNamara, by contrast, had precisely the style Kennedy liked and responded to (and had wrongly assumed he'd find in someone so experienced as Rusk). McNamara had a fast, analytical mind, 1 . . . 2. . . 3. . ., speed-reading skills, terse phraseology, an appetite for argument, wide-ranging curiosity, an intent, direct, "no nonsense," yet informal approach to the matter at hand. So did JFK. Their operating styles meshed. McNamara joined the intimates with whom Kennedy spoke in half sentences, following each others' minds faster than speech. Rusk got left out.

Rusk's reticence seems to have stemmed from genuine distaste for aspects of this operating style combined perhaps with underlying shyness and a mind, however good, that did not move as fast or roam as far on short notice. Rusk was affronted by Kennedy "seminars," mingling cabinet officers and staffers in free-form discussion where no protocol applied: one voice was as good as another. Rusk shrank from that—and from the challenge it implied. As secretary of state, he thought it his duty to have the last word of advice and to speak it to the President in private. But he found it hard to claim and take what he wished to receive as a matter of right. Seeking the appropriate occasion, he often missed the bus. Rusk also conceived it his duty, oftener than not, to let his State Department staff voice views regardless of his own, lest he stifle ideas and energies. If someone had to shut them up, it should not be "their" secretary, better McNamara. Against his own aides Rusk sometimes urged McNamara on, to the latter's bemusement—and Kennedy's.

The sources for Rusk's reticence were veiled from Kennedy. Rusk, a loyalist to his fingertips, suffered bruised feelings in silence. JFK for long was unaware that his own style played a large part in causing Rusk's behavior. More and more the President leaned on McNamara in tandem with Bundy. This was ad hoc reaction, not deliberate design. By way of compensation it worked, after a fashion, but a lot of things dropped through the cracks, not least with regard to Vietnam, where a clear, consistent, orchestrated, diplomatic alternative was neither conceived nor debated in Kennedy's time.

Poor interlock of operating styles, like Rusk's with Kennedy's, may be inevitable when men who have not previously worked together are thrown together. The best way to treat that is by diagnosis and reform or resignation, not by ad hoc adjustment without consciousness of causes. Kennedy had actually arranged to have a diagnosis made; he read it a week before his death. By then he was almost three years into his administration.

That's a record you should try to beat.

3. Filling Jobs Because They're There

The White House counsel's job has an instructive history. The title "special counsel" was originally invented by Franklin Roosevelt in 1941 for Samuel Rosenman whom he persuaded to give up a judgeship and come to Washington to undertake assignments like the ones he'd done for FDR in Albany ten years before. These combined preparation (or coordination) of major speeches and messages to Congress with review of draft executive orders, proposed bills, and enrolled ones, superintending OMB's [Office of Management and Budget's] legislative clearance work and carving out items of White House concern. Rosenman was thus astride all the chief avenues (except press conferences) by which the President staked out and publicly defended policy positions. Incidentally, pardons came through Rosenman as well, but other legal matters he left largely to Justice, which was jealous of its status as the President's legal adviser.

When Rosenman departed after Truman took office, the latter did not fill his post until a rush of enrolled bills at the next session of Congress made the vacancy painfully obvious. Clark Clifford then was hurried out of uniform and into Rosenman's place. Clifford quickly picked up all the threads and wove them into the chief policy job on the White House staff (mostly domestic but foreign too whenever he could manage to insert himself) as well as a center of strategy for the 1948 campaign, in which he also served as chief speechwriter.

Clifford was succeeded by Charles Murphy in 1950, but their bundle of assignments broke apart when Eisenhower came in. Most policy tasks and speechwriting went elsewhere in a hierarchically organized staff. Eisenhower did appoint a special counsel who clung to what he could: executive orders, enrolled bills, the link to OMB, and pardons with a link to Justice. In 1961, Kennedy, who had been briefed on the earlier history, gave the title to Ted Sorensen with a mandate to restore its former character. Sorensen did. He was at once chief speechwriter and what would now be called "domestic policy adviser" (with a staff of three) and, after the Bay of Pigs, a member, in effect, of NSC. Legal advice, in stricter terms, he left to Justice.

In 1964, after Kennedy's assassination, Bill Moyers succeeded to Sorensen's work. A year later Joe Califano succeeded Moyers (who became press secretary). But Moyers (not a lawyer) had not taken on the title, and before Califano arrived it had been given, being open, to Harry McPherson. He kept executive orders, shared enrolled bills, had a frequent hand in speeches, and alongside Califano played a somewhat independent role.

When Nixon was elected, [H. R.] Haldeman, seeking a job for John Ehrlichman, a lawyer, gave him McPherson's, shorn of speechwriting, as counsel (the title "special counsel" went to Charles Colson who was, indeed, special). Within a year, Ehrlichman took on functions akin to Califano's in domestic policy. At that point he acquired a new title, and the counselship was filled as a subordinate legal job by John Dean. In 1973, amidst Watergate, Dean was replaced, and the job took on a distinctive cast as the President's own lawyer, also helping White House aides with legal problems like conflicts of interest. This continued under Ford.

The Carter people found this pattern and took it for granted. They continued it, indeed elaborated on it, with associate counsel often intervening in the substantive concerns of other staff. When Lloyd Cutler took the job in 1979, he added a certain luster and accepted a series of ad hoc tasks which leave the role remote from Clifford's or Sorensen's, not central but high level and liable to be either a fifth wheel or a loose cannon, especially when buttressed by staff.

Does the President need "his" lawyer in the White House? Acting as such, distinct from aides who happen to be lawyers? Separate from the legal staffs at Justice? Since Watergate, maybe so. But if so, it is not because the last administration left the title and the slots behind.

Whether or not you decide you need a counsel-and-associates, the question is worth asking and answering before you appoint one. Note also how speechwriting got divorced from substance. Here too is a question to ponder.

The point can be generalized: most White House posts have histories that do not show on their surface. Many had their origins in felt needs of past Presidents now met by other means. You cannot fully know your needs until you have experience. Meanwhile, it is well not to assume without inquiry that experience will cause you to want everything you find there, not at least just as it is.

Once filled, jobs are hard to drop.

The opposite side of this coin is that vacancies ache to be filled. Twenty years ago Kennedy was persuaded, soon after election, not to fill the post of OCDM director (now defunct) because he might wish to reorganize it out of existence. On the day before inaugural he yielded to pressure to place a helpful (but talkative) mayor; this job, being vacant, was vulnerable. He let him have it. JFK then discovered, to his chagrin, that one aspect of the job was statutory membership on NSC, a reason why the NSC, as such, met rarely in Kennedy's years.

So there isn't much time to inquire.

4. Slashing Jobs Too Soon

Three weeks after inaugural in 1961, a White House press release announced abolition of most staff positions and machinery, notably the Operations Coordinating Board, built up in Eisenhower's time under the NSC. The secretary of state (said the release) would take over the functions. The thought that NSC staff ought to be reduced was part of the conventional wisdom of the time, but this went farther, faster than reformers then were urging. Abolition by press release was odd to begin with; it reflected the fact that no staff work had been done, or agreements made, on how State was to do that takeover: when, where, with whom, by what procedures, all unknown. The theory was that State would start from scratch. It didn't. What was dropped was not, in fact, replaced during Kennedy's time. This did not harm the President directly. What it did do was deprive subordinate officials at State and in the military of the regularized flows of paper which conveyed to them administration decisions and gave them a crack at draft plans. These often were fuzzy in written form; never mind, they were at least tangible. They also conveyed an assurance of due process: addressees could feel they had a firm place in the system. After abolition of the paper, along with the committees which produced it, all became uncertain at those middle levels. For a while this played havoc with morale. It contributed also to muddle.

In 1977, somewhat similarly, seeking economies and ways to demonstrate that they'd reduced the White House staff, Carter reorganizers shoved together most administrative services of the Executive Office agencies, OMB and White House alike. One result, predictable but unexpected, was to reduce the supply of messengers available for White House trips downtown and to the Hill. One of the many reasons why Carter's congressional relations were beset by fumbles in his early months was that the White House messenger service, long a wonder of Washington, had been discombobulated by attempted integration with the messengers of OMB and other units.

Moral: Think twice about the changes for the sake of change (or of publicity). Incidentally, regarding that consolidated Office of Administration, grab hold of it and get it looked at closely in your interest.

5. Forming Cabinet Councils

FDR was the first to preside over something approaching contemporary "big government." Early on he experimented with continuous, collegial consultation among traditional department heads and chiefs of emergency agencies, all grouped around him in a National Emergency Council. This was complete with a secretariat headed by Donald Richberg, then one of his chief assistants.

The NEC met from 1933 to 1936 (when Roosevelt lost interest). At the start he did most of the talking. He had had more Washington experiences than almost any of the others, and he used the council as a means to make his attitudes, priorities, and inclinations plain across the upper ranks of his administration, kindling loyalty and a sense of sharing, if not always acquiescence. He also tried to use the council in discussion of administration strategy, and of its options on specific issues, but he did not do so long. Roosevelt found few members ready to engage with one another on their own pet projects, which they wished, rather, to discuss with him alone. He also found them ready to mousetrap him if they could by their agreement, when they could agree, on matters he wished rather to keep open or to stay above. ("It's all your trouble, not mine," he once said about legislation *they* were pushing.) Further, he increasingly found council meetings boring: large numbers doing show-and-tell while eyeing one another to see who'd be first in line for private talk with him when they broke up.

Also, FDR began to find the council leaky, and when later he reverted to department heads alone, meeting with the traditional cabinet, Vice President Garner (or so Roosevelt thought) conveyed every word to the anti–New Dealers in Congress. After 1937, Roosevelt did no serious business in cabinet meetings.

Thereafter, FDR seems never to have used a cabinet group for anything he could get done through staffs or departments taken one by one, ad hoc, as he saw need, not in orderly fashion.

Truman came in critical of FDR's disorder and set out to govern "through" the cabinet, meeting frequently for serious work. In eighteen months his disillusion with the cabinet as a council was complete. The egoism and parochialism of most members startled him. His later cabinet meetings were increasingly *pro forma,* and he did most of his business with individual members and small groups tailored to matters at hand. In the process, Truman grew quite philosophic about the parochialism of department heads, granting them to be as much the servants of congressional committees as of him.

Eisenhower, who may have had fewer illusions to begin with, tried considerably harder to make cabinet meetings meaningful. He saw in them ways to build team spirit, bolster flagging energies, and bring his personality to bear upon department heads, some of whom he otherwise would rarely meet. He thoroughly appreciated how domestic cabinet officers enjoyed telling the home-folks about White House briefings on the international scene. Aside from these, his cabinet aides searched hard to find agenda items cross-cutting parochial concerns from State to Agriculture. Often, they did not succeed, and Eisenhower's meetings could be boring too.

Successive Presidents since Ike's time have had comparable experiences. By all accounts, Kennedy and Nixon may have been the most impatient, Johnson the most overbearing, Ford the most attentive, and Carter the most courteous. But for them all the cabinet meeting came to be a duty, not a pleasure, nor a source of collective wisdom, nor even a spur to consensus. Smaller groups on separate subjects were preferred in every case, in Nixon's the smaller the better.

Nixon was the first to try to cut cabinet numbers to manageable proportions for a consultative group, while simultaneously giving members superintendence of the rest of government in such a way as to accord them White House status, line and staff at the same time. As announced in January 1973, four top White House assistants (one serving also as the secretary of the Treasury) and three White House counselors (each also heading a department), along with the attorney general and the OMB director would develop policy and oversee operations across-the-board: staffing the President where he was interested, substituting for him otherwise. Group meetings were apparently *not* central to this plan, the second five (and everybody else) would deal with Nixon mostly through the top four. However that might have worked out, the scheme was overwhelmed by Watergate and was abandoned three months after it got started.

Press stories now suggest that Governor Reagan's Sacramento cabinet can be reproduced in Washington by adaptation of that Nixon scheme. Maybe so, but look at the two closely; they may be less alike than forms suggest. Even with numbers, nine greatly exceeds six if meetings are in view.

And the intended corollary of Nixon's nine was a scatteration of tested loyalists across the departments, as undersecretaries or assistant secretaries, helping to ensure implementation. The link of the nine to those loyalists and the persistence of their loyalty are matters of theory, not practice. The experiment ended too soon. Congressional and interest group resistance scarcely had time to show. Shielding, if any, for Nixon himself from resultant rows scarcely had time to be tested.

6. Linking Foreign with Domestic Perspectives

The original precursor of Zbig Brzezinski or Henry Kissinger as national security adviser was Harry Hopkins in World War II, helping Roosevelt manage his relations with Churchill and Stalin, while also helping Navy, War, and State deal with the President. The Hopkins role varied from month to month; FDR sometimes used him as alter ego, then switching, kept him at arm's-length—in classic Roosevelt style—but nobody was closer or more nearly privy to the President's concerns in foreign policy and in the conduct of the war—or indeed in domestic policy and politics: throughout, Hopkins helped write major speeches of both sorts. This he could do the more readily because he had won his spurs with Roosevelt and in policy on the domestic side, building up an engine of the New Deal coalition, WPA [Works Progress Administration].

Before the war, Roosevelt had made Hopkins secretary of commerce to broaden his appeal for a possible run at the Presidency. Illness put an end to such ambitions; Hopkins was a sick man through the war and died soon after. But this background made him unique among foreign policy advisers then and since: once he got the hang of his new work, he had a range of interests and experience as wide as presidential duties (which do not respect distinctions between foreign and domestic, or policy and politics). Like Roosevelt himself, Hopkins changed his focus with the war but kept his footing in domestic affairs.

By Kennedy's time, a generation later, the statutory NSC (a cabinet committee with staff), the Department of Defense, an enlarged State Department, the CIA, and the alumni of war government, returned to private life, had grouped around the President a foreign policy establishment, long on varieties of expertise in every sphere *except* domestic policy and politics.

Kennedy's first serious encounter with inherited experts and his own fresh appointees from that establishment produced the "Bay of Pigs," an American-mounted exile invasion of Cuba, which failed in embarrassing fashion.

The failure and its causes are brilliantly arrayed in a new book by Peter Wyden, *The Bay of Pigs* (Simon & Schuster, 1979), which ought to be required reading for transition teams. It is distinctly a transition story; Kennedy, who blamed himself, with reason, came to regard it so.

One of the things this episode taught Kennedy was his vulnerability when military or diplomatic advice, and foreign intelligence, came at him independent of domestic and political perspectives. Lacking magic to turn McNamara, Rusk, or Bundy into a Hopkins, Kennedy devised a substitute. His brother—the attorney general, formerly campaign manager—and Sorensen, his domestic-adviser-cum-speechwriter, were added to the inner circle with which JFK henceforth reviewed all major diplomatic and defense decisions. (He also added his secretary of the Treasury, Douglas Dillon, a friend and Eisenhower's undersecretary of state to boot.)

Unlike Jimmy Carter's recent chief of staff, Hamilton Jordan, Robert Kennedy and Sorensen cared as much for the substance of domestic policy as for the calculations of electoral politics. This gave them double weight and the President double duty when he brought them into national security affairs. From his standpoint the arrangement seems to have worked well on discrete, defined decisions and on crisis management, less well to monitor the work flows in between, when those part-timers were preoccupied by all their other doings.

For Kennedy's successor Lyndon Johnson, it could not work at all: RFK and Sorensen dropped out of the inner circle. Johnson fashioned for himself a sort of compensation, another circle, private, occasional, informal, wholly unofficial, and linked to the officials largely through himself. The occasional group included old Washington and Democratic hands: Clifford, Truman's counsel, and Mr. Justice [Abe] Fortas, Johnson's friend since New Deal days. A difficulty with this group was that however sensitive their finger-tips on the domestic side, their views were not informed by close acquaintance with the flow of information on the foreign side. Clifford, long a relative "hawk" on Vietnam, evidently altered that perspective quickly after his immersion in the cables when he replaced McNamara as secretary of defense.

Nixon, taking a different tack, put an elective politician, Melvin Laird, in Defense, a friend without foreign experience, William Rogers, in State, and proceeded to run his own show from the White House utilizing Kissinger to build a staff with capability for independent diplomatic action. But Nixon prided himself on personal expertise in foreign policy as well as politics and saw himself, it seems, quite capable of bridging the two to his own satisfaction. Johnson and Kennedy sought substitutes for Harry Hopkins. Nixon evidently sought to play the role himself.

What substitutes do you seek? How improve on theirs? In today's scale and complexity, one person can't do it alone.

7. Holding Staff Size Down

Watergate afforded classic illustrations of the reasons why it pays to limit numbers of professional staff entitled something "to the President" or otherwise entangling his House in their business: high-level loose cannons like Colson, second-level self-seekers like Dean, third-level eager-beavers like [Egil] Krogh, fourth-level fumblers like [E. Howard] Hunt, all with energy enough and time to exercise bad judgment on what they conceived to be the President's behalf. All were identified as "White House," yet most were out of sight, too many for him (or for his chief of staff) to keep under surveillance, let alone control.

The Carter staff suggested further reasons why it pays to limit numbers. There were more leaks and gripes and anti-Carter sentiments from inside White House precincts than old Washington hands can recall from ever before. The sources seem to have been mainly second- or third-level national security and domestic policy aides. Some were almost openly in business for themselves. Their rampant indiscretions may relate to lack of human contact down, resulting in a lack of loyalty up. Nixon was an isolate but recognized the need to "stroke" subordinates; Carter did not. However that may be, there were a great many to stroke: up to three times the number under Johnson or Eisenhower.

The growth in numbers of professional staff at the White House since Nixon's arrival there is partly the product of technology. The Press Office is a case in point. Partly it is the product of an upward creep in outside demands on long-established functions like congressional relations. Partly it is the product of new claims upon the Presidency acceded to without much thought for consequences. Public "liaison" offers numerous examples.

In Nixon's time, following earlier precedents, a "wailing wall" entitled Public Liaison was built for women and minorities and staffed by some of each. Some twelve professionals—a group as large as FDR's entire wartime staff—were holding hands and doing case work by Ford's time. Carter simply replicated this group to begin with, then later found a different purpose for it and restaffed it around Anne Wexler as a purposeful lobbying effort on behalf of key legislation, aimed less at Congress itself than at those who might influence Congress from around the country. The wailing wall, displaced, arose again piecemeal, with individual appointments which will tempt you now as vacancies. Beware. Caseworkers in the White House do not help the President to get his own work done. Why, then, are they there?

Twenty years ago, when asked for advice on the point, I argued successfully that Kennedy *not* make Louis Martin a White House "adviser for Negro affairs," but rather, if a named contact were needed, put him in the National Committee for the purpose. There should be at the White House, I suggested, blacks (and women, Jews, etc.) with real jobs to do, helping the President do his, and these aides could serve simultaneously as symbols, or in times of stress, hand-holders. But a wailing wall as such belonged elsewhere.

Such advice seems reasonable still (at least to me), and it may well have counterparts elsewhere within the White House, NSC, or the Domestic Policy staff.

The point is not to arbitrarily cut staff just for the sake of cuts. Carter's people tried that with some ill effects. Rather, it is to reserve space for later, deliberate growth, meeting priority needs as you experience them without markedly enlarging present numbers. For these are already vulnerable to Nixon's troubles, and Carter's.

Public liaison aside, Ford's White House was more sensitive than Carter's on this score. Congressman [Dick] Cheney or Jim Connor can tell you.

Memo 14
Transition Planning during the Campaign

For: Paul Brountas
May 25, 1988

Here are a few further thoughts on "transition planning." These are first thoughts not last, but at least they put a gloss on my top-of-the-head reactions at the close of our conversation the other day.

1. A small Transition Planning Group, with you, perhaps, as chair, *pro tem,* and Susan [Estrich] as a member, could be draped around John Sasso as full-time planner. He needs a close associate by the way of someone recently experienced and informed in Washington: insightful, flexible, discreet, and ego controlled. On reflection, I withdraw the notion of the two new recruits to the campaign. They are indeed good and fit the bill, but if they are to be prospectively of maximum use to Michael [Dukakis] after election, they should win their spurs in the campaign and with fellow campaigners during it. That precludes sitting on the sidelines as a postelection associate planner.

Jim Baker never could have made a bid to be or been accepted as the Reagan chief of staff had he not spent the months from July to November 1980 campaigning.

So, who's the "associate planner" for that little group? Some time ago, Hale [Champion] mentioned to me the possible utility, for a rather different but compatible role, of his former general counsel at HEW [Department of Health, Education, and Welfare] (in 1977–1979), Dick Beatty, now a partner in a major New York firm. To me, that's an attractive thought on three scores: the man himself, his location in anonymous New York, and his law firm, where discrete things can be done discreetly. But don't take it from me, check Hale.

There are of course others, not many but some, and more likely in Washington than New York, for instance Stu Eizenstat.

2. This "associate planner's" tasks are two, as I see it: (a) to help John [Sasso] get up to speed on Washingtonian timetables, personalities, procedures, *and* pitfalls, congressional and executive; (b) to help get straight, and put straight, the choices, both of process and of people—and of PR too—the governor need make between election and say Thanksgiving. And at only slightly greater leisure come the ones between Thanksgiving and Christmas. The first set of choices, chronologically, should be ready for Michael Election Day itself and the day after. These will be mostly immediate procedural and staffing choices plus public statements. A week later is soon enough for him to start considering most post-Thanksgiving matters!

3. A Sasso-Beatty planning team (or some such), with you and Susan kept abreast, needs a discreet, energetic aide or two who could be shaken loose in one law firm or other for research and miscellaneous chores. *Period.* Before election, the team could commission confidential inquiries or seek advice from others, and they should, but *quietly* (which limits sources and numbers). After election, as fast as possible, they themselves should become advisers to the nascent White House staff, which by their efforts would be quickly taking shape around the governor. Except where needed to postpone decisions he wants postponed, or otherwise to divert public attention, the "transition group" and that planning team could be out of existence by early December, Christmas at the latest.

This assumes that Sasso then goes to the prospective White House staff either as chief of staff or as some sort of counselor (or assistant) to the President for political affairs, a role legitimated by Carter-Reagan practice. Michael need not *now* decide which, but he should decide whether (in his private mind, not publicly) before Sasso even starts the planning task.

As for Sasso's associate—Beatty or the like—one condition of his taking on that task should be that he would not be interested in any full-time job within the White House or the wider

Executive Office (or the cabinet, for that matter, if you don't think this ties Michael's hands unduly). You and Sasso need no self-denying ordinances (and please don't issue any); this relative stranger does, lest media speculation and potential rivals eat him alive.

4. I stress people and process over substance now in part because the very terms of the election, and the international context, along with foreign and domestic reactions to both, will condition substance for the near term in a host of subtle ways. They require a commensurate response, the terms of which are hard to foresee in detail, especially by campaigners absorbed in a still shorter-run activity, trying to get elected.

Had JFK endeavored to plan cabinet appointments and economic policy, or the timing of both, in any detail before 1960's election, I'm almost sure he wouldn't have foreseen that the day after he would find he'd won by merely .06 of the national vote and set off a flight of gold! Yet those things influenced a multitude of subsequent decisions.

Besides, a golden haze descends upon the brotherhood and sisterhood that fought the rough campaign (however close), altering judgments of issues and people. Part of [Jack] Watson's trouble in November 1976 was that Carter apparently had grumbled to him about [Hamilton] Jordan, [Jody] Powell, [Stuart] Eizenstat, et al. in October: led the lad astray!

5. In these respects the transition experience after Michael's Massachusetts reelection seems to me to offer imperfect analogies. I urge you to look at the differences hard. Besides these, I (in my ignorance of your experience) think I see at least the following:

(a) Eight years in Washington, especially Reagan's eight, is a lot longer than four in Massachusetts.

(b) And Michael isn't coming back, anyway (nor would he to Carter's regime if he could).

(c) Congress may be harder to deal with than the great and general court—at least there's nobody there equally able to deal. Mobilizing pressure from home districts becomes indispensable to ad hoc coalition-building.

And rarely has there ever been a "honeymoon" in congressional terms, save superficially to reflect (and wait out) initial public approval. (Maybe that's like the state house?)

(d) Washington is "Hollywood East," as Dick Darman once phrased it in 1979 (before Reagan)! At all times TV dominates the media scene, both more formidable and more manipulable from the White House than the State House (barring blizzards).

(e) Then there's defense and diplomacy: the world impinges through the cables and intelligence—and TV's minicameras linked to satellite transmission (next to the bomb, the most awesome of technologies in White House terms).

Such things suggest to me three rules of thumb for transition planning:

First, try to master what's there before tearing it down. (And knowing what was there eight years ago may not suffice.) This means quick, quiet study, even of Reagan procedures, even policies, both before Election Day and especially right after.

Second, staffing and procedural innovations in the White House and Executive Office under Reagan should be looked at hard before being abandoned or arbitrarily changed. Suitably adapted, some may advantage his successor. At least, Michael should have a conscious choice! Personnel selection and media relations are two such—and Anne Wexler's brilliant innovations in public liaison, ten years ago, are a reminder that hard looks should extend back to Carter's time, maybe even to Ford's (e.g., General [Brent] Scowcroft at NSC).

Third, especially in media and congressional relations and most especially in national security affairs, many choices should be made no sooner than the President-elect acquires the experience for informed, personal judgment. He won't have it at the start. (Not even if he thinks he does.) Isn't that the biggest difference between resuming the governorship and now? This counsels hedging some bets.

JFK abolished Ike's entire NSC process and staff system by press release; it said State would take over, but there was no plan for that: abolition followed; re-creating didn't. The Bay of Pigs, to some extent, was a by-product. Then, armed by experience, Kennedy et al. worked up substitutes to suit him.

6. One further thought: Michael's transition group, however composed, will need to swallow hard and constantly remember who in government can help them most: the people there now, on the Hill and downtown. When it comes to White House matters, that means Reagan's people, the two Bakers [James and Howard] and Darman above all (I have a little list of others also, mostly former students). Whether they, Jim Baker aside, are prepared to be helpful prospectively, before election, I don't know. But there's precedent for it running back to 1948. Afterwards, in any event, my own experience both going out and coming in suggests that they'll be eager to be helpful in all ways. They'll mostly be so anxious to hand over to people who've learned from their mistakes and appreciate their triumphs. Human. Worth exploiting to the full. Transition advisers rarely do. (I didn't: too busy and too confident a new world's aborning.)

Enough. If you want more, I'm happy to supply it; I promised Michael to be helpful if I could be. But it's your nickel. In these matters I've found the soundest rule is "never volunteer."

Memo 15
"Lessons" for the Eleven Weeks

For: Robert B. Reich
August 13, 1992

1. Organize the core of the White House staff by or before Thanksgiving and set them to superintend the preparatory work on things the President-elect himself has to do or approve first. They desperately need to gain experience before January 20 in working with him and with each other in the new roles they are assuming.

2. Appoint the bulk of department heads by mid-December and get them to D.C. in touch with outgoing counterparts and civil servants. Give them qualified initiative on assistant secretaries and below, subject to White House veto. (Doing it the other way gives the White House control but for what? In time they all go native anyhow.) But make it an active veto; pushing the personnel operation into high gear, with an adequate fence around it. Beware congressional aides since each has an agenda item all his own, or his boss's. Keep actual personnel screening and reviewing outside Washington. The "fence" can be in Washington.

3. Do not appoint "task forces" except on substantive issues of immediate concern where advice is really needed, or big shots have to be conciliated. Above all, leave organizational task forces to cabinet members' initiative (with White House staff concurrence).

4. Return most of the federal funds [for the transition] to the Treasury (reduce the debt a bit), thus avoiding temptations to spend it on campaigners, raising their hopes for permanent employment, creating a prima facie case for that, thereby unleashing intense jockeying for advantageous access to agency payrolls. That jockeying will badger civil servants, distract incoming White House aides, and subject new department heads to constant observation. (The President-elect himself won't know how bad it is for everybody else.)

5. Decide the fields on which you're going to be "bipartisan"—e.g., jobs, investment, taxes?—and then pursue the leaders of the opposition party on the Hill as though their names were Vandenberg and yours Truman (but your own party leaders need to be kept informed).

6. Keep the President-elect out of Washington, except for frequent visits, but put him and his staff someplace the press corps will enjoy (Nixon: New York; JFK: Palm Beach, New York, Hyannis). Not Plains, Georgia. Don't play softball with reporters and insist on winning.

7. Appoint a visible and trustworthy liaison with the outgoing administration. Surround him with sufficient staff in Washington for press and personnel to serve the fence function, keeping the multitudes out of the real staff's hair. Have him make sure the outgoing White House orders what you need from executive agencies for interim management (including space, transport, FBI clearances, White House passes, etc.).

8. Be immensely courteous to the outgoing White House but don't agree to share responsibility for anything.

9. And don't prematurely announce actions the President-elect can't actually take before 12 noon on January 20. Remember Carter's $50 tax cut: announced in December, withdrawn after inaugural!

10. As December turns into January, fill most of all the subordinate posts in the White House itself. There are too many there, no

doubt, but it'll be a year or more before the President-elect knows which he'd dispense with and why. The time to reorganize and shed staff is immediately after reelection (as FDR and Nixon found).

Memo 16
Role of the Vice President

For: Reed Hundt
October 6, 1992

One point I didn't get to make is more affirmative (!). Our man [Al Gore] has one thing to offer the President of enormous and unique utility, if the latter's wise enough to see it and remember it in office. Everybody else around the White House, his wife aside, is an appointive assistant with experience primarily in foreign or economic or social policy or legislation or campaigning, or media. Most of them will have assignments reinforcing that experience. Yet the President's choices, from his own perspective, mingle foreign, domestic, legislative, administrative, and political considerations and are drenched with public relations. For him, there are no *ors*. Moreover, his experience, the source of his own insights, is political in a different dimension: he has run the gauntlet of election and in his first term faces running it again. That's all to the good, that's the essence of his accountability. But nobody around him shares this special vantage point except the Vice President, at least this one, who in this instance has both brains and character, brings his federal experience to the table, and sees still more gauntlets ahead (not 1996, 2000!).

What a prospective asset to the President! Somebody with whom he genuinely can kick around choices in the same terms as are relevant for him himself: a very special sounding-board. And the VP offers the additional asset that he can't be fired, which guarantees a certain independence of judgment (unlike the White House staff, which tends to be more royalist than the king). Ordinarily that's thought of as a vice, but rightly viewed, it gives to the VP's advice some of the same value one gets from a wife, or a brother like Bob Kennedy.

If the President sees this "rightly" and takes advantage of it, then the VP will wish to play up to it, by being constantly informed and constantly available on everything the President's about to ponder. That means avoiding or deferring long-term assignments which immerse the VP in a heap of second-level issues marginal to the West Wing. Of course, if the President doesn't use him so, long-term specialization may be the way to go. (Writing books, another form of that, seems good to me, more so the more I think of it.)

Hence, this becomes the VP-elect's first big choice—and it depends upon an estimate of what the President-elect will really want and how he will behave once he has settled in, with jealously protective aides around him.

If the President is really smart enough to figure out—and follow through on—the utility of the VP to him as fellow-politician, hence as special sounding-board, then that's the only kind of specialty I think the VP ought to court (at least until his independent future comes much nearer).

The stake for this President is great: everybody else in the West Wing of the White House will probably be classified as either "foreign" or "domestic" and personally has not faced sudden death by ballot box. Outside the White House, friends who may have done so can't keep current on the cables or the papers or the meetings, day by day, and so won't know the fine detail just when they need to know it.

The VP, if he wants to—and has associates as his eyes and ears in NSC, cabinet councils, OMB, and Capitol Hill—is better placed than any outside politician to be abreast of the detail whenever his advice is either sought or volunteered. But he cannot hope to keep abreast at once of presidential detail and of frequent foreign trips or constant pulls or pushes from the interest groups surrounding competitiveness, space, technology, ecology, whatever, for which he has been delegated some degree of formal, public responsibility.

Alas, the President is bound to find a foreign funeral he cannot attend—and send the VP instead. Once begun, such things are hard to stop or ration: they are so convenient for the President.

And no one but the President, repeatedly insistent, keeps the VP in the loop on his decisions. Alas, what history suggests is that the President too frequently forgets, or never grasps, that his behavior is the key to the other's performance. A budget director once said to me:

> Thank God I'm here and not across the street. I've plenty coming up to me which keeps me going in to see the boss, by rights, whether he calls me or not. But those poor fellows over there (he spoke of senior White House aides), if the boss doesn't call them what can they do but sit?

The risk in ducking long-term assignments is that the boss won't think to call (except *pro forma*). The risk in taking such assignments is that none is likely to enclose such action-forcing issues, of such moment to the boss himself, as budget directors stand astride! And if one asks for such as those, one joins the ranks of [William H.] Seward in 1861, or LBJ in 1960, or Gerald Ford in 1980: almost certain to be told "no" by the incumbent or prospective President on staff advice. Ford, in 1976, did give to Nelson Rockefeller the chairmanship of the Domestic Council (as it then was), whereupon staff practice shortly turned the role into a dud.

So the key here is the President. History's discouraging. Yet the Vice Presidency, in its executive dimension, is still new, still evolving, still relatively plastic. Our prospective VP has far more to offer than most before him (Humphrey and Mondale possibly excepted), while the campaign has combined them in an unprecedented way. Is it feasible to build on that? Think! Check! I can't help with that.

Memo 17
Rules of Thumb (Based on Historical Experience)

Attachment to Letter for Reed Hundt
October 6, 1992

1. The VP reminds the P of his mortality; the P reminds the VP of his dependency.

2. The White House staff lives in the present, the VP's staff in the future.

3. The one is more royalist than the king, the other more papal than the Pope; protectiveness induces paranoia, each about the other.

4. In return for White House space and other perks, the modern VP never differs with the P, unless by prearrangement, when third parties are present.

5. The VP can't be fired, but the P can ignore, or haze him—and, if the P, then staff will too—with relative impunity.

6. The only thing more frustrating than being bypassed is to have one's advice heard, pondered, and not taken.

7. The one thing more frustrating even than that is to attend all the meetings, hear all the briefings, and be morally certain you'd do better than he.

8. Still, it's a great introduction to the executive branch, provided you're good at spectator sportsmanship—and patient beyond belief.

9. Yet wiggle room is low and press attention high; previous senators, it seems, have frequently felt caught, confined, constrained, and sorry for themselves.

10. Professors don't raise students to become VPs. Better they should play piano in a house of ill-repute. Humphrey and Bush may well have lost their crown jewels; Mondale his independence; Johnson took to drink, etc. (2000 could compensate, but will I live that long? More to the point, can he?)

Memo 18
A White House Title for Hillary Clinton?

For: Professor Diane Blair, University of Arkansas-Fayetteville
December 8, 1992

As promised, I enlarge herewith on the views I gave you Friday night, in the course of the campaign managers' conference at Harvard. I'd like to see Mrs. Clinton carry off the designation we discussed, but having read the applicable statute, I'm now dubious on grounds of public relations.

I don't know Mrs. Clinton, but we have friends in common, and they've told me something of her role, both past and current, as a close adviser to him [the President-elect].

In my understanding this is a role wholly consistent with the sort of help a President needs sorely but almost never gets—namely responsible, informed advice on choices across the board of policy, personnel, and politics, from a perspective as wide and electoral as his need be, and focused on his agenda. A President's desk is no respecter of distinctions between administrative and political, economic and social, domestic and foreign, military and civil. Yet except for the Vice President and for the chief of staff (sometimes) and occasionally one or two others, the entire body of White House and Executive Office personnel, to say nothing of the departments, consists of appointive aides with narrower perspectives and separable agendas built into their jobs (as well as into their time-horizons).

I cannot overstress the gap between a President's necessitous perspective, stemming from his job, prospects, place in history, and that of almost all others, stemming from theirs.

Mrs. Clinton is set, it seems, to fill a great part of that gap, and she seems thoroughly qualified to do so by professional attainment and experience, as lawyer, politician, and wife. What a good thing for him!

The trouble is that no first lady has performed as such before in a complete and overt fashion. To be sure President Carter says in retrospect that he sought his wife's advice on everything, while Nancy Reagan evidently was a tiger at the gates about her husband's public reputation, place in history, and speaking schedule. But as I get it, neither was regularly, effectively in the loop of advice coming from others, so each depended on her husband or a friendly White House aide, or on the media, to know enough to be effectively of use when asked, or to raise questions in a timely way. When Mrs. Carter, seeking background information, occasionally joined a cabinet meeting, there were hostile leaks to the press. When Mrs. Reagan pressed Don Regan on a personnel decision, that leaked too.

Eleanor Roosevelt did have an overtly public role, acknowledged, attacked, and defended. She moved about the country as her husband's "eyes and ears," and sometimes as his political delegate. She championed social causes of particular concern to her. She lobbied him both publicly and privately and also was a hairshirt, his nagging social conscience. She wrote a syndicated column. She had her own press corps (consisting of women reporters, a boon to them in those days!). In twelve years, Mrs. Roosevelt thoroughly established the precedent of first lady as an independent actor on the Washington stage, as well as presidential partner in some aspects of politics, and only incidentally a traditional hostess. But the one thing she didn't do was serve as close adviser across the board.

"First lady" as an (unofficial) title was the only one Mrs. Roosevelt had, aside from "Mrs. FDR," except for a brief stint as cochair of civil defense early in the war. Earlier this year, most commentaries in the press, both pro and con, assumed a role for Hillary Clinton on the Eleanor Roosevelt model, with "children's issues" paramount (to be sure, an expansive array). Since the precedent is there, were that assumption correct, I'd see no need for a separate title. "First lady" sufficed before (however silly on its face) so should again. It won't spare Mrs. Clinton criticism any more than it did Mrs. Roosevelt. But any sort of activism assures that, and anyone close to a President is fair game for the shafts aimed indirectly at him.

The question of title arises precisely because the scope of Mrs. Clinton's role, its comprehensiveness and confidentiality, could well appear so different as it evolves. If I have it right, she'll need to be in the loop of information flowing to the President on virtually every issue. This means that the White House staff must serve her routinely in some ways no previous first lady has been served before: keeping her abreast not only of the choices facing him, but also of the substance and the politics in all the options put to him by others. She cannot give useful advice unless she knows what he knows when the time comes—and unless she knows his timing. (Historically, a characteristic trouble with advice from friends and family has come down to that: not knowing, in context, what's timely.)

But if the whole staff serves her so, the press will learn of it. And if she joins in meetings with other advisers, or with cabinet members, or with congressional leaders, as she'll want to do and ought to do for the sake of good advising, that also will reach the press. And since the role is new, at least in these dimensions (Reagan and Carter are only precursors), publicity risks imputations of illegitimacy or usurpation.

To meet those risks it seems to me imperative to be upfront about Mrs. Clinton's role, the President's desire for it, her capacity to play it, and the gains he expects from it for himself and for public policy.

Governor Clinton made a good start on this at his press conference after dining with the congressional leadership. One way to be "upfront" is to continue in that vein from time to time, and casually be first to tell the press what she is doing and what staff is doing for her. There will of course be criticism as time goes on. But as long as the telling is his, and she's doing what he says he wishes, neither imputation is likely to flourish for long. This doesn't mean he won't be criticized for bad judgment, and she too. But that comes with the territory, whatever they do or don't.

Would a separate title help? In my personal opinion (no better than anyone else's) yes, if announced in the roster of the White House staff, the President's personal advisers—provided the Nepotism Act, so called, doesn't cloud things more than the title clarifies them.

Unfortunately, that's a closer question than I thought the other evening. I've now looked up the statute (5 U.S.C. § 3110, December 16, 1967): LBJ's revenge on Bobby [Kennedy] it appears; I've no recollection; perhaps Warren Christopher does. It flatly prohibits the appointment (among others) of a President's wife to a position under his jurisdiction or control. The penalty for violation is loss of pay.

Is designation by descriptive title of advisory duties without pay tantamount to "appointment"? I doubt it. Would anyone sue to find out? I doubt that too; a Circuit Court has held that there's no private cause of action (*Ligmonqelli v. Postmaster General*, 707 F.2d 368, 371, 9th Cir., 1983). But making that clear to the press would take some doing, and Mrs. C's detractors, to say nothing of Republicans on Capitol Hill, might well raise a hue and cry, readily countered but perhaps not so easily forgotten.

This leads me to think that the title you and I liked, "counselor to the President," might be more trouble than it is worth, precisely because it has been held by others in previous administrations and thus could be more readily made to appear a "position." How about a title never previously employed, to my knowledge, in official parlance: "adviser to the President"? ("National security adviser" is a newspaper invention cultivated by Henry Kissinger and successors since. Their actual title's been "assistant to the President for national security affairs" and will, I hope, remain so.)

If the distinction between "designation" and "appointment" should be thought to need more stress, then how about "first lady and adviser to the President"? The point could be made when this was announced (at the head of the list of White House aides) that the additional designation simply was a clarification, intended to make sure that everybody understood the President expected this first lady to continue after January 20 as before—not by way of "pillow talk," but rather as a matter of acknowledged consultation on a par with that of other senior persons in his entourage.

The counterargument is that "first lady" alone can stretch to cover anything and cannot be improved upon by adding extra words. No other title is necessary and none carries more weight, once it has been acknowledged what the President wants done and that she's doing it.

If there are to be no extra words, it becomes all the more

important that the message be conveyed in other forms, not only by Mr. Clinton's statements but also by strong signals. One such is appropriate inclusion in the White House listing of the *Congressional Directory* and the *Government Organization Manual*. Another such is a West Wing office. Whether small and supplementary to the traditional East Wing suite or large, in exchange for it, Mrs. Clinton will need the convenience of a desk and telephone and private meeting place close to her husband's office and to other senior aides. She shouldn't have to walk a long block between meetings; they don't. And all Washington would notice: As George Ball once said, "Nothing propinks like propinquity."

Given the complication of 5 U.S.C. § 3110, I cannot be as firm as when we talked about the usefulness of separate title or the rightness of "counselor." It becomes a close question of public relations, too close to resolve from this distance.

I continue to believe, though, that the function she's performing now, wide-ranging close advice, should be continued and, if so, should be acknowledged, calmly, casually, recurrently—no mystery about it. That's the essential thing.

Let me add, incidentally, that I'm of precisely the same mind about Al Gore and Warren Christopher, should he or someone like him become chief of staff. (Should I add Bruce Lindsey? I don't know enough about him.) Here are more advisers whom the President-elect may trust enough and calibrate well enough to keep around him as close counsel with broad range, cultivating a perspective as wide (or almost) as his own, and in Gore's case nearly indistinguishable for at least four years.

To have his wife and Al and somebody like Chris [Warren Christopher], all at once, all utilized, makes Governor Clinton rich indeed in what to me are the most critical of presidential staff resources. He'll need them. For, unless I miss my guess, he may find that the domestic issues, where perhaps he feels most certain of his ground and his new team, will have to take a relative back seat to foreign issues crowding in upon him from the moment he takes office. And our national security establishment, from which he's bound to draw the bulk of diplomatic and defense advisers, is notorious for failing to quite fathom policy-political considerations or the weight of personal responsibility that Presidents themselves experience.

If so, generalist advisers of the broader sort are to be badly needed. Three is none too many! In that regard, Clinton's made some good choices (starting way back). The issue of a title for his wife is but part of a larger puzzle: how to make the most of just those choices.

Memo 19
Further Thoughts on the First Lady

Supplement to Letter for Professor Diane Blair
December 9, 1992

Last night I showed a copy of my previous memo to my wife [Shirley Williams], asking for her untutored reaction out of nineteen years in Parliament, six in cabinet. She's British, not American, but an elective politician to her toes, so I thought her reaction worth having and now think it worth reporting.

She says, in effect:

(1) The PR problem with the Nepotism Act is determinative, so forget an advisory title—and don't attach one to first lady; that'll court ridicule, cartoons!

(2) But the person in question does need a separate public role legitimating closeness to her husband on policy choices. Otherwise, every elected politician in the country, to say nothing of the nonelected, will resent that closeness. Who elected her?

(3) In Britain, an answer would be the chair of a "Royal Commission on the Status of the Family," or some such, with a long-term assignment and provision for short-term findings or status reports. In America an almost exact counterpart could be created privately by a consortium of foundations which invite your friend to take the chair. Mobilize Carnegie, MacArthur, Ford, and Rockefeller! (Isn't Chris [Warren Christopher] chairman of the Carnegie Board?) There are precedents: e.g., the Wickersham

Commission, privately funded in Herbert Hoover's time.

(4) There's hardly an aspect of public policy, even foreign policy, not touched by considerations of family life, structure, prospects. Thus, when the commission chair is seen in or around her husband's office, there's almost always a rationale—"What's a family angle here?"—to ease instinctive resentment. Won't cover everything, or always, that's too much to ask, but a good wide-angle start.

(5) Without some plainly reasonable, separate professional existence, she's unduly and unfairly vulnerable. No matter how qualified to be a general-purpose close adviser, if that is all she's seen to be and do, resentment will rise higher than it should—from inside the Beltway still more than from outside.

One woman's opinion only, but I thought you should have it.

Part 4

The Author's Reflections

Neustadt Advises the Advisers in 2000

It is hazardous to be President-elect of the United States for the first time. All such are inexperienced, since nothing previous encompasses the unique job of President. So all are vulnerable to arrogance in ignorance, their own or that of their associates. It is scarcely less hazardous to advise somebody of that sort, or a selected surrogate. The chief difference is this, as John F. Kennedy once put it: "The President has to take the responsibility. . . . [A]dvisers may move on to fresh advice."[1]

As one such adviser, whose advice to many persons under varying conditions you have now sampled above, I think that I am reasonably qualified to testify about the hazards of advising, the conditions for it, and perspectives native to incoming Presidents.

Since 1960, I have kept a somewhat disorderly file, "Transition Correspondence," into which I have dumped letters and memoranda written under various circumstances, in response to varied inquiries from a variety of would-be members of incoming administrations, Kennedy's, Carter's, Reagan's, Clinton's, and not "incoming" after all, Governor Dukakis's. My custom was never to volunteer, lest nobody be listening, but to answer all questions, since the questioner might care. When Charles O. Jones was writing for the Brookings Institution his fine recent book on transitions, I lent him the whole lot, which is how they found their way to the American Enterprise Institute and the Brookings Institution's Transition to Governing Project, of which this book is a part.[2]

It cannot be an accident that Jones, this volume's editor, selected thirteen of those memos that to my certain knowledge were read by JFK at the successful close of his campaign—or by James Baker, Ronald Reagan's designated chief of staff, after the close of theirs—and selected only four memos (and two supplements) solicited, more distantly, by friends of other candidates. In the latter category are many more that never reached their presidential targets, or, like these four, may have or may not, without my knowing one way or the other (and without my asking, since it was not my affair how friends conducted their relationships). Clearly, Jones found most useful, for present purposes, advice that had at least been seen by those of assured relevance in new administrations.

But it is wholly accidental how I came to advise Kennedy, while Baker's request of me came through, or at the instigation of, two Kennedy School colleagues, both Republicans, one of them very close to him. That Harvard link was but an accident of timing, since they shortly left the school for Washington. The accidental quality of Baker's case is therefore quite straightforward.

In Kennedy's case, the accident takes longer to explain. In 1957, I became an occasional consultant to Senator Henry M. ("Scoop") Jackson's Subcommittee on National Policy Machinery (which changed its title every Congress, thus becoming known by his name only, as the "Jackson Subcommittee"). In the summer of 1960, Scoop was asked to chair the Democratic National Committee—a sort of consolation prize for being passed over as vice presidential candidate. Just that spring I had published *Presidential Power,* and eight years earlier had served in the most recent Democratic White House, President Truman's. Late that summer, Jackson—ever a conscientious doer of chores assigned him—asked me to prepare a memo on the transition tasks that would impose themselves upon his candidate before inauguration, January 20, 1961, if Kennedy should win the forthcoming election. This I gave Scoop on September 15. It is included in Part 2 as memo 1, "Organizing the Transition."

Unknown to Jackson, Clark Clifford had seen Kennedy in August at Hyannis Port, had warned him of transition problems, and, in return, had been given by the candidate an assignment not unlike the one the party chairman had given me. This I knew because George Elsey, Clifford's assistant in Truman's time, had been recruited to help Clifford, and I had been recruited to help Elsey—which I had promised to do once I completed my task for Jackson.

In the third week of September, Jackson took me and my memo to JFK at his Georgetown house, as he passed through Washington on a campaign trip. Kennedy read the memo with close attention, as occasional questions testified (in a display of speed-reading which left my jaws agape). He then turned to me, said he wanted more, especially about White House deadlines and organization, and told me how to get it back to him. A bit startled, never having met him before, I improvised a quick test of his seriousness. Knowing that it would surprise him, I asked, "How do you want me to relate to Clark Clifford?" He looked at me sharply and responded, "Don't. I can't afford to have only one set of advisers on anything—if I did that I'd be on their leading strings." As Arthur Schlesinger, Jr., wrote four years later, recounting that episode, "After Kennedy said that, the author of *Presidential Power* was thereafter on his leading strings."[3]

So I had to phone Clifford, back off from helping him, and agree only to give him copies of what I wrote for Kennedy once the latter had received originals, with time to read them. So I subsequently did. (Clifford did not reciprocate, which scarcely is surprising.)

There followed, before election, the next memos in Part 2, including the appendixes on Rooseveltian practice. On November 4, with the election four days off, I was put aboard the candidate's private plane, the *Caroline*, to deliver these new memos. When I did so, I urged Kennedy not to talk and not to read, to save his voice for a major speech that evening in Chicago, and his attention for the last days of campaigning. "These memos," I said, "are to be read on Election Day; before then, just try not to lose them." Half an hour later, he burst out of his partitioned-off, private cubbyhole to give his secretary something. As he did so he said to me, "That Roosevelt stuff was fascinating, absolutely fascinating." So he had disregarded my injunction and turned first to the historical material, a characteristic choice, as I belatedly discovered.

On November 9, after Kennedy's late-night, paper-thin electoral victory, I had a call from Schlesinger, who was with him and his staff at Hyannis Port. Arthur told me, with some asperity, that Kennedy had come charging out to his postelection staff meeting, issuing a series of assignments and instructions, while clutching in his hand a sheaf of papers, which, on inquiry, he identified as "memos from Professor Neustadt." Arthur wanted copies, which I promised with no thought of actually complying.

Later, in his initial postelection press conference, JFK spoke of meeting the next week, at Palm Beach, with his "transition advisers, Clark Clifford and Professor Neustadt of Columbia University [where I then taught]." Kennedy knew me so little that he gave my name its German pronunciation, which my great-grandfather had been forced to shed when he first reached America. Never mind: That is how I learned I was, and would remain throughout the weeks ahead, an active adviser, producing the rest of the Kennedy memos above and more specialized ones besides.

What could be more accidental?

When I first went to Palm Beach, a week after the election, I found the nascent White House aides assuming that I would join them. But this I could not do without becoming a competitor and thus spoiling my usefulness as everybody's friend, consultant to all, conveyor of experience from Truman's time and earlier. That usefulness was by its nature temporary, bound to wane quickly, as the White House staff took shape and aides gained confidence. But while it lasted, my utility could not help but be great, and I was fired by the chance to make that sort of contribution. Only a major staff position astride some key action-channel flowing toward the President could have tempted me to do otherwise, and those were either spoken for, or I had my own candidates whom I preferred over myself for rational reasons. Besides, my family had been promised a sabbatical in Britain the next academic year, and the best way to ensure that was to remain on the sidelines. So I did.

I had to enlist Clifford's aid to get JFK's entourage to believe me, but with his help they were at length convinced. I was allowed to play the waning part. I have always been pleased with myself that I had objectivity enough to do it.

What I learned from that experience, and from lesser opportunities later, is to take seriously the hazards in transitions to which advisers are prone, no less than those afflicting advisees. Of the latter I have previously written in chapter 11 of *Presidential Power,* first published in the edition of 1980, and I shall enlarge on some of them below. But on hazards for advisers I have up to now been silent. So I give these pride of place.

Hazards for Advisers

In advising on presidential transitions, risks for the adviser can be summarized as ignorance compounded by inhibitions and haste. While *ignorance* can mean not knowing, it can also mean not comprehending what in some sense one may know.

"Not knowing" has been characteristic of all transition studies that purport to advise nominees of both major political parties. There are, of course, some general pieces of information that affect both, like expiring legislation, or jobs on Schedule C, or White House salaries, office space, clearance procedures, et cetera. And White House history is certainly important for both, though rarely covered in enough depth by such studies. I sneer at none of those. But "bipartisan" studies rarely stop there. Rather, they go on to questions of appointment, policy, and management, which at the start of new administrations will not, and cannot, be the same for the successful candidate of either party. The authors of such studies in the past have evidently thought that they had no choice except to disregard the idiosyncratic in those respects. Whether they literally did not know, or simply felt they could not say, is immaterial. That disregard rendered their reports of marginal value to actual victors.

Such was the case in 1960 with the pioneering report of the Brookings Institution, grandfather of them all. It was read, if not by JFK, then by at least a couple of his aides. It contained some information of undoubted use to them and was, perhaps, a handy check upon the likes of Clifford and me. But its lack of sensitivity to circumstances of the Democrats, and to Kennedy's in particular, limited its relevance after his election.[4]

More specifically, not knowing, in the sense of literal ignorance, hampered my first attempt to give JFK genuinely helpful advice as he began to think of cabinet choices. In my memo of November 3, 1960, "Cabinet Departments: Some Things to Keep in Mind," I covered State, Defense, Treasury, Justice, Commerce, and Labor, with notes on some major agencies and promised a later memorandum on the rest of the departments. But the truth is that I made that promise because I could not think of anything much to say about them, and in fact the later memo was never written. What I had known of them in Truman's time I had forgotten, and I had paid too little attention since.

Why not temper ignorance with inquiry? Why not go to Washington and ask around? That raises quite another risk, the hazard of exposure, hence the loss of trust by advisees, compromising the adviser's usefulness to them as he becomes a plaything for the press. That hazard has grown enormously since 1960, but even then I was hypersensitive about it.

Kennedy had no prior aquaintance on which to base any trust in me at all. The only people I could talk to, so I felt, were the few on Jackson's Senate staff whom he had told of my assignment and one on Kennedy's Senate staff. I had known the latter as an undergraduate, when he interned for a summer at the Budget Bureau, and we had worked well on matters of mutual concern. But they were of no help to me on Agriculture or Interior or Transportation!

The departments I did cover in that November 3 memo also illustrate the shading between sheer ignorance and the subtler phenomenon of incomprehension. Not knowing Kennedy's family, nor having been involved in his campaign, I did not comprehend the blend of competence, intimacy, and trustworthiness embodied for him by his campaign manager and brother, Robert. A close reading of the press might have done that for me. Mine was, evidently, not close enough. Had it been, I would have realized that such a one was indispensable inside the government and would have made a place for him in my design. I did not.

JFK chose Justice for his brother, which I probably would not have done in any circumstances. For both of them and for the government it proved an excellent choice, no thanks whatever to my advice.

On the borderline between not knowing and not grasping what I might have known was my insistence in the 1980 memo for James Baker, "Historical Problems in Staffing the White House," on stringing out the story of the White House counsel's office. To be sure, I had once worked there. And to be sure, I had long deprecated its conversion by John Dean, in Richard Nixon's time, into a sort of law firm for White House aides (or Presidents) in personal trouble. But by hindsight, such a law firm seems a pretty good idea in the face of scandal-hungry media. By the same token, I would have done better to devote at least as much space to State-Defense relations and the evolution of the NSC, especially in Truman's years.

As things evolved from 1981, it would have done Baker more good to learn about the falling-out of 1950, between Dean Acheson and Louis Johnson (who decreed that no one in the Pentagon should speak to anyone at State without his express permission), and its attempted resolution by Averell Harriman, than to learn all I offered about how there came to be so many lawyers at the White House. Baker learned soon, on the job, about the crucial importance of NSC staff and its leadership. He learned enough to try to take the lead himself in 1983. Would that he had succeeded! It is a mark against my comprehension that the White House history which might have alerted him still sooner is missing from that memo.

By those remarks I do not mean to equate relevance with fortune-telling. I could not have been expected to peer far into the future. Transition advisers to Presidents, however, or to their chiefs of staff, ought to be able to anticipate at least the faint outlines of future problems from present evidence. Of that there was no lack at the end of 1980, with respect to the emergent Reagan White House and foreign affairs, or to relations of Defense with State. By hindsight it is clear both that I failed to tell Baker some of what he needed to know and that some of what I told him was unlikely to matter much, known or not.

To lack of knowledge, incomprehension, and also inhibitions toward one's advisees, add carelessness induced by haste. That is a fourth hazard for advisers. To exemplify: When Clark Clifford was named Kennedy's liaison to the Eisenhower administration, in November 1960, he agreed to give the White House a note of introduction for each Kennedy appointee, as selected. The White House, in turn, would arrange for the new person to receive services and office space from the retiring incumbent. I agreed to make this real, with respect to each incoming White House aide, by giving Clark a single sheet explaining who each opposite number was in the outgoing administration. I still recall my pleasure when, on January 3, 1961, I wrote my sheet for McGeorge Bundy, the incoming assistant to the President for national security affairs, and listed fully five outgoing Eisenhower aides for whom he was the counterpart.

But that was in error. There was also a slice of a sixth, a big slice: the unpublicized part of the job of the staff secretary, General Goodpaster, in liaison with the intelligence community as well as operationally with Defense and State. This I knew perfectly well. Indeed, I had alluded to it in another memo as recently as December 23. I also knew, for he and I had talked of it and Kennedy assumed it, that Bundy would pick up those duties. But somehow I forgot to flag that in Clark Clifford's introduction of him to the Eisenhower administration. Accordingly, the military aides in that administration signified to their successors that those functions of the general were theirs to grasp. Kennedy's incoming military aide acted accordingly.

It then took Bundy some four months of unremitting effort to get liaison arrangements into his own hands. He told me of the effort, but he never charged me with the error. Yet it was my fault, by way of inadvertence, no doubt under pressure of time.

Hazards for Advisees

The hazards for those to whom advice is offered, the advisees, so to speak, are not the same as those for advisers, although in some respects quite similar. What haunts the advisees are haste, hubris, and newness—the sort of newness generating the incomprehension that is fueled by inexperience.

Haste is a hazard for the objects of advice—for Presidents-elect and their immediate associates—no less than for would-be advisers. The eleven weeks between election and inaugural are eased, somewhat, since Kennedy's time, by an additional three weeks until the annual messages, which now go up in February, not January. And Congress customarily goes out of session, after convening January 3, until the message season. But cutting against those easements are the complications now attendant on presidential appointments, thanks to the Ethics in Government Act, elaborate procedures, and too many lawyers. Secular changes in media coverage add to the complications. So do federal dollars for transition staffs and "teams."

Time is still woefully short in which to build a White House staff, select a cabinet, shape an initial legislative program, review the budget, reassure civil servants, connect with congressional leaders, woo the press corps, and present a public image different from—more national, less partisan—that in the run-up to election. Haste is unavoidable.

So is hubris, at least in the form of arrogance and innocence combined, which I describe in *Presidential Power.* That description was inspired by the sight of Jimmy Carter taking office. The later sight of Clinton doing so makes Carter's behavior seem almost modest. The arrogance, at best, consists of thinking that "we won, so we can, while they didn't and couldn't," amplified by almost certain overestimation of the Presidency's potency. From any other office in our political system, it looks comparatively strong, much stronger than it does from inside. Thus, those about to climb inside for the first time are almost bound to overestimate the power that will soon be theirs. In that consists their innocence.

Complicating tendencies toward hubris in those terms is the inevitable inexperience, which makes so many of the choices facing Presidents-elect virtually incomprehensible to them. Kennedy did brilliantly, during the eleven weeks, especially in the public relations of converting a barely elected young Catholic into President of all the people. He stumbled only after that in his encounter with the Bay of Pigs. But even Kennedy, from a political family and with fourteen years of congressional experience, could not have been expected to grasp every nuance in the choices I so confidently put before him by memoranda. That I evidently held the expectation suggests still another hazard for advisers. I underscore that now. But Kennedy, as advisee, was subject to the very different hazard that his legislative experience left him no purchase on some executive issues.

I think particularly of the proposition that he should appoint a "special assistant to the commander-in-chief–elect," a temporary aide, drawn out of the intelligence community (for reasons of immediate convenience), who could bring him up to speed before January 20, both on how the community actually produced the daily briefings he would get from the CIA and what, by way of special operations, might be cooking there that his administration would inherit. I had also recommended the retention, at least temporarily, of the CIA's director, Allen Dulles. This Kennedy implemented on his first day after election (along with that other Republican and household word, J. Edgar Hoover). But that temporary aide would free the President-elect from undue dependence on Dulles, who could be shelved later, if the President then wished, once the new administration was entrenched.

Ten days after the 1960 election, I found myself at Palm Beach, trying to explain, across the dinner table, what that temporary aide with the fanciful title was for and what he was supposed to do. Not having been inside the government for eight years, I was starved of pertinent illustrations. A Jackson Subcommittee colleague had some, but that was no help to me. He was not in the room. Kennedy was, but simply could not get it. He saw neither the point nor the need. And I could not enlighten him in a convincing way.

Finally, I said, "Senator (not yet having been chosen by the Electoral College, JFK refused to be called President-elect), there must be someone in the intelligence community you know well enough to trust. Let me take this proposal to him, get him to vet it, and come back to you about it independently; if he agrees with it, he should be able to explain it to your satisfaction." Kennedy thought for a moment, then responded, "OK, take it to Dick Bissell: He's the only person in the intelligence community I know well enough to trust."

I did so. Bissell told me he agreed with me, might undertake the task himself, was scheduled to see JFK, and would discuss it with him. I left it at that and heard no more from either man about it. Four and a half months later I discovered, with the world, that Bissell had been planner and director, under Eisenhower and since, of the Cuban-exile landing at the Bay of Pigs—the very sort of thing my fancy transition aide was to arm Kennedy against! But the latter could not get it; inexperience stood in the way—and also barred his way to candidates more qualified in the peculiar circumstances than was Bissell.

Another instance may be startling to those who read my memo on the NSC, "National Security Council: First Steps." Kennedy and Bundy had not been in office many days when they put their heads together and decided to abolish the Operations Coordinating Board (OCB). That was foreshadowed in my memo and also in a recent report of the Jackson Subcommittee, but neither dreamed of anything as precipitous as Bundy and his boss cooked up. The board they abolished by press release—a charming idea but not government—which also announced that the State Department would absorb its functions. They did not discuss that with Jackson, or with me, which certainly was their right, but neither did they discuss it with the secretary of state. Like everybody else, he read it in the newspapers.

There were no accompanying presidential documents, nor even formal notice to the newly abolished staff, and nothing had been done by way of staff work to prepare a substitute. Bundy and the President, I take it, simply assumed that [Dean] Rusk would figure out what was needed and put it in place. Had the latter had the temperament of Robert McNamara, his colleague at Defense, conceivably he might have tried to do so. Kennedy, who appointed them both without knowing either, might have been confused on that score at the outset. But Rusk being Rusk, he waited to be consulted and instructed by the President. He never was, so nothing was put in the OCB's place until JFK and Bundy learned from their failure at the Bay of Pigs. They then evolved procedures through Bundy's office.

Inexperience and the incomprehension it engenders are rendered the more dangerous for newly elected Presidents and their close aides by unfamiliarity with press relations as embodied in the present White House press corps. Even so, it never occurred to me to write a memo on press relations to JFK. He and his campaign aides seemed to be doing fine in that regard. There seemed to be more genuine affection for him among members of the press I knew than ever since Franklin Roosevelt's time, and he, like FDR, seemed to regard himself as almost one of them. A love affair was going on in 1960, and one did not have to live inside the Beltway to perceive it.

But that was at the tag-end of the era before television came to be the leading medium and before the vast expansion of the White House press corps, which Kennedy's own performances helped bring about. It also was before the big news organizations made a practice of changing White House correspondents with each new administration. Further, it was well before a segment of them came to be celebrities in their own right, made so by TV exposure.

All such changes make it difficult, two generations after Kennedy, for any President-elect to come up smelling like a rose from an immersion in his own transitional relations with the press. The press corps, newly constituted after the last election, is competitively tense about relations with incoming aides and with their boss. The celebrities among them are competitive, as well, in wanting service fast and hot. The oldsters among them are thoroughly disillusioned by constraints imposed since Nixon's time upon their movements and their contacts. The newcomers are shocked to discover these and can become disoriented by the gaps between the prestige that their posts command in theory and the confining realities of their daily work. Finally, they all simmer at their own necessitous dependence on the presidential entourage to pass along the handouts, stories, backgrounders, and leaks, and above all the pictures, which their own professional advancement may require. "News management" à la Reagan began with these.

Resentments are the greater because regular press conferences at stated intervals—reliably unvarying—were abandoned in Nixon's time, as I recall, and have not been steadily resumed yet.

Charming the media, which Kennedy managed with minimum effort in 1960, is harder to do under modern conditions and chancier, too. I once asked a member of the press corps in President Clinton's time, why, from the moment he took office, they appeared to cut him so little slack. My respondent grew intense: "He lied to us on his first day and has done so ever since," was the reply. Correct or not, it was heartfelt. In that atmosphere, making headway with reporters cannot help but be hard.

Physical conditions during the transition weeks often add to the hardship, although Kennedy's conditions did not. He spent his eleven weeks, with reporters in tow, rotating among Palm Beach, Georgetown, midtown Manhattan, and Hyannis Port, all places the reporters (and their families) liked to go. Ronald Reagan's reporters did almost as well, if a bit more laboriously, criss-crossing the continent between Southern California and Washington, D.C. But Carter spent weeks in Plains, Georgia, with reporters parked at a motel in Americus, and Clinton spent still more time in Little Rock—a city, one Northern reporter told me, with all the verve of downtown Worcester, Massachusetts, on a Saturday night!

Press convenience cannot be allowed to dictate the President-elect's locale. But lack of concern for their enjoyment betrays unfamiliarity with the exacting media relationships ahead. It also can betray exasperation at what may well have been ghastly media episodes during the campaign just concluded. And the exasperation may be heightened by the sense, "Screw them, we've got them now!"—the hubris of the innocent again. Carter and

Clinton, by all accounts, offer cases in point. It took them time in office, on the job, to realize that what they had learned of press relations in state capitals and also on the campaign trail did not equip them either to deal masterfully with White House reporters or to use what they knew advantageously in "managing" news through that press corps.

Inexperience for incoming Presidents, and especially for close associates, is complicated further by what was meant as a reform, in Kennedy's time, but subsequently became a curse, namely federal funds for transition assistance during the eleven weeks. That was, in part, my doing. (With every new administration I feel guilt for it.) In the winter of 1960 I was troubled to discover that my friend, David Bell, the incoming budget director—whom I had backed enthusiastically for the job—was constrained to spend over a thousand dollars of his own money to house himself in Washington, where he had to be, in the weeks before he joined the federal payroll on Inauguration Day. Columbia University had put me on a three-month salaried leave, and Jackson was defraying out-of-pocket expenses. But Dave had had to resign from Harvard, and his expenses could be charged to nobody but him. The same was true of everyone asked by the Kennedys to join their New Frontier.

After the inaugural, David and I discussed this situation with an eye not to the past but to the future. (For those of us from academia, a thousand 1960 bucks was not small change!) Presently, he took it up with JFK, who brought it to the notice of the Speaker of the House, Sam Rayburn.

The upshot was a law and a quadrennial appropriation covering expenses for both incoming and outgoing regimes between election and inauguration (or in the case of outgoers, until the former President's relocation). The sums involved were modest to begin with but have grown with each successive changeover. In 2000, the incoming President is slated to receive $12,000,000. What is the money spent on? Mostly on personnel—on the David Bells, to be sure, but preponderantly on others with no paid counterparts to speak of in 1960.

That money is a bonanza: three months of extra pay for campaign aides, supporting them while they endeavor to insert themselves into the government, and up to three months also of expenses for partisan supporters with some claim to expertise, assigned to "teams" reviewing policies and management in the departments. All those people race to Washington, where most of them could not afford to go in previous Novembers. They settle down there, tripping over one another, getting underfoot, sometimes trampled, now and then triumphant.

The whole crowd is a latter-day (paid!) equivalent of the patronage seekers in the nineteenth century. It puzzles and sometimes hampers the relative trickle of David Bell–equivalents, the designees for top jobs in departments and agencies. And it ages, irritates, sometimes confuses, even alienates their prospective civil servants, about whose feelings the incomers typically do not care. As much as a year later they will—and wish they had.

The crowd has to be managed lest it get in the way of serious preparation for governing. That adds a new dimension to transition tasks. But it tends to be mismanaged by most nascent administrations when there is a party change. The most nearly successful effort, to date, was made in 1980 by the chief aides to Ronald Reagan, who (perhaps not quite consciously) divided up the work of herding the crowd, on the one hand, and preparing to take office, on the other.

The herding is effortful stuff, hard work, though not high-level, and it should not have been imposed on people with too much to do already and too little time to do it in. During 1992, I urged somebody around Clinton to have him graciously return the money to the Treasury as a gesture to reduce the budget deficit. Of course, that was not taken seriously. And now it is too late: The budget is in surplus!

In 1976, reportedly, Carter thought it altogether reasonable that some, not too many, not more than about 120, of his most deserving campaign aides should get three months of federal pay in Washington until they could be eased onto some permanent payroll or other and given a chance to show what they could do. Reagan and Clinton seem to have thought likewise, if more expansively, when their own transitions came. Why not? Campaigning is prolonged and arduous, stretching back two or more years. Only a very few can be assured of long-term places in the new administration. There are not enough of those to go around, and there is far too much competition from among professional middle-class adherents on congressional staffs, investment houses, law firms, public-interest groups, and think tanks, who wrote position papers while the campaigners campaigned. So give the lads their holiday and let them rummage around!

To do otherwise would seem ungrateful indeed, not only to them, but also in the eyes of their elected candidate. Yet, if he knew enough to ask himself, "What's in it for me and my close aides?" he would be bound to answer, "Nothing"—except possibilities of noise to complicate his early media relations. And if he knew enough to derive that answer for himself, he would regret that Congress had thrust funds upon him. What good is money that does no good for him? With scarcely eleven weeks, his nascent staff surely lacks time to play Santa Claus to those most committed to him. Without the money, no issue of ingratitude could come between him and his young campaigners. None did with JFK; he had no public funds.

But no one who has not lived through a presidential transition from the topmost place, or close to it, would ask such a question or answer it so. Inexperience, and its accompaniment, incomprehension, rule.

To sum up, the transition hazards that afflict a President-to-be and his immediate associates are born of haste, hubris, and the unfamiliarity native to newness. The counterparts for their would-be advisers are sheer haste, again, plus inhibitions natural to aides, unrealistic expectations of their masters, and their own gaps in understanding, the fruits for them of ignorance, compounded by limited empathy.

Incomprehension is a critical phenomenon for both. The Presidents cannot fully grasp what they are getting into. The advisers, typically, cannot wholly make up that lack, in part because they do not fully understand their Presidents.

Experience, of course, is the great corrective. For most problems of transition, it used to be resorted to with ease, at little cost: just wait for the inaugural! But that was in the olden days, before the Great Depression, when new Presidents had nine months of office before Congress hove on the scene; months in which to update, months in which to start to comprehend, months in which to breathe, experiment, prepare, and learn. All that is gone.

Contemporary transitions take place under different conditions, in different anticipations, framed by the terms of our Constitution as amended in 1934. To those I now turn. They are what make the hazards so particularly hazardous. They are what give the eleven weeks their bite.

Conditions

All the memoranda in this book address transition in what I have elsewhere termed the "narrow" sense, confined, that is, to those eleven weeks before inauguration. Actually, transitions in the wider sense of learning time last longer, through the first years after inauguration, while the new President and his associates experience for the first time all characteristic aspects of the office, down to and including the "midterm" congressional elections. In *Presidential Power* I have offered illustrations of necessitous and painful presidential learning on the job—the Bay of Pigs, the Lance affair, Iran-Contra, others.[5] But for present purposes, commenting on the limited, if vital, tasks of taking office, and on memos pitched to them alone, it certainly is right to use the narrow definition, the eleven weeks.

That time span is the product of the Twentieth Amendment to the Constitution, adopted hastily in 1934 to guard against any recurrence of the horror of the year before, when a national banking crisis came smack in the middle of the sixteen-week interval between November's election and the March 4 inaugural specified since 1787 by the Constitution itself. The amendment also eliminated the anomalous "lame-duck" session of Congress—superseded by November's election—which previously had met from December (when it regularly convened) to March 3, the day before the new President was sworn in. Instead, by the amendment, the new Congress would meet on January 3, seventeen days before that swearing in, now specified for January 20 of the year after election.

Under the old scheme, the new President had nine whole months from March 4 to the following December before encountering the new Congress elected with him (unless he chose to call it into special session). Now, under the amendment, that new Congress would be sitting, already organized, awaiting him impatiently on Inauguration Day.

The unintended side effects on "narrow" transitions nowadays are obvious. Indeed, were Congress still absent from the first nine months of a new Presidency, the eleven weeks before inaugural would seem to be a happily long playtime, instead of a scarily short interval for effortful preparation. But nobody thought about that in 1934. Nor did anyone experience it until 1952.

FDR's three-plus terms and Harry Truman's nearly two—after succeeding at the former's death—delayed until Dwight D. Eisenhower's first election an initial test of the revised transition period, shortened by five weeks and shorn of the traditional nine months to ease into office without Congress (unless and when wanted). Since Ike, six other elected Presidents have taken office under the revised conditions: Messrs. Kennedy, Nixon, Carter, Reagan, Bush, and Clinton. An eighth will do so on January 20, 2001. So far, only one of those has been of the same party as his predecessor; the rest embodied a full party changeover. That is the condition all the memos in this book address.

Only George H. W. Bush, and by next year perhaps Albert Gore, Jr., or their closest aides, could enlighten us on the exceptional condition of elective takeover without a party change. My own experiences have not reached that far, except for fleeting thoughts in 1952 about the possibility that Adlai Stevenson might follow Truman—about which there was neither time nor need to be other than fleeting.

And if there were to be, instead of Gore, a second Bush, the first one would continue to stand alone in that regard. Judged from afar in 1988, transition hazards then were superficially eased, although not altogether escaped, while one fresh hazard supervened for both the President-elect and his advisers: How to make substantial changes in both policies and methods without seeming abrupt about it, or inconstant, or inconsistent, given one's former fidelity to one's predecessor? That question takes its modern bite from the contemporary press corps, and from sometimes-sentimental publics, vis-à-vis former Presidents, and from potentially obstructive party colleagues, clinging to prior policies and offices.

Leaving that exceptional circumstance aside, in the usual case—complete with party turnover—three aspects of the eleven weeks deserve more recognition than transition studies in the past have accorded them. First is what I might call a time warp in advising. Second is a vastly useful, generally unused, outpouring of advice for incomers by outgoers. Third is the inadequacy of institutional memory, and of resorts to it (such as it is), by either new officials or surrounding reporters. Let me comment on those in turn.

Time Warp for Advisers. First, the time warp for advisers is sufficiently illustrated by the situations of Clark Clifford and me in 1960. Kennedy was using us because he thought we knew something of use to him. Indeed, we did. What we knew derived from our experience in the most recent Democratic administration. But eight years of Eisenhower experience had intervened. Yet inhibitions, coupled to discretion and constraints of time, limited our ability and stomach for investigating all of that. We were not wholly ignorant about it. Clifford had dealt frequently with Eisenhower and his entourage. I had studied from outside as closely as they would let me. Yet our primary reliance was upon our deeper knowledge of our own administration, eight years old. Hence the "time warp."

I vividly recall the evening in December 1960 when JFK asked us whether he really would have to give fifteen-minute interviews to every senator or congressman or assistant secretary who sought him out. Someone had told him that. Clifford responded gravely that indeed it was the case, that half of Truman's days were taken up that way, as had been Roosevelt's before him. Kennedy was appalled by not alone the time commitment but also the prospective boredom.

Seeing that, I urged him to take his own reaction seriously—it was his time, after all, perhaps his most precious resource—and to innovate, giving good reasons publicly and preparing to ride out the rap.

But sitting in our time warp, Clifford and I were both wrong. It turned out that Kennedy could dispense with the traditional fifteen minutes on demand, as he did, yet take no rap. Why not? Since Eisenhower's heart attack in 1955, and then his ileitis operation in 1957, both ends of Pennsylvania Avenue had grown accustomed to more selective and restrictive meetings with the President.

If the next Republican President-elect were to ask David Gergen to play something like a Clifford for him, recognizing the superb public relations of the early Reagan years, and the extraordinary "news management" in which Gergen had taken part, the chief risk for the latter would be inattention to the transformation in communications since, and the effects on White House capabilities to do as Reagan had done, in Reagan's way. Gergen being Gergen, a studious person and experienced in Clinton's first term, also, he probably would come as close as anybody could to avoiding a time warp. But the effort involved in doing so will be obvious to anyone who compares the press corps, TV networks and their news, local TV, cable, satellites, commuter radio, the talk shows, and the nascent Internet of twenty years ago, with "now," whenever that may be.

To match Reagan's methods through transformed technology is hard even to think about, much less accomplish, as Clinton, who has tried it, seems to have discovered. Escaping a time warp in those terms is no light matter.

Even when sitting Vice Presidents manage to get themselves elected President, as Nixon did after an eight-year hiatus, and George H. W. Bush did in immediate succession, updated comprehension is not guaranteed to either them or their advisers. Vice Presidents and their assistants live in a twilight world of delegated powers and covert competitions. Psychologically and practically, it is a wrench to move up suddenly—soon to sit in the Oval Office, live on the family floor—after a long, exhausting interval campaigning on one's own. When they contemplate that, I am told, vice presidential minds tend to snap back to what seemed to have gone wrong in their predecessor's transition and how to improve upon it. The time warp then renews itself.

Admittedly, we lack sufficient instances to justify generalizations. A Gore transition, if it comes, might teach us many things—though if it did, not even a third swallow makes a summer.

Advice from Outgoers. Moving to the second matter on which I wish to comment, the matter of advice from outgoers, the goodwill of those leaving office for their successors-to-be, regardless of party, must be seen to be believed. But rarely is it seen in time to do the newcomers much good. I first encountered the phenomenon in 1953, when Gabriel Hauge, designated to be the economist on Ike's immediate White House staff, visited Dave Bell, who had a somewhat similar assignment on President Truman's staff. The time was early January, perhaps two weeks before the Eisenhower inaugural. Since I shared an outer office with Dave—

my small inner office was linked thus with his big one—he asked me to sit in.

When Hauge arrived, we seized upon him with enthusiasm amounting almost to desperation. By trial and error we had learned so much about good staff work for a President and how to do it. We did not want our learning to be wasted! Hauge was our first and so far only avenue to those who would now follow us. Never mind that Bell had been on loan to Adlai Stevenson, campaigning against Eisenhower. Never mind that I had been with Truman as he roamed the country, slashing Ike for "moral blindness." Those things were in the past—for us. We now were in the business of handing on the sacred office of the Presidency to a bunch of novices who had never before been there. Oh, how we ached to help them learn!

Hauge, it appeared, was startled by our earnestness. Judging by his eyes, as they glanced around the room, it soon became apparent that his interest was in Bell's office, not in indoctrination by the likes of us. Perfectly politely, he broke off as soon as he could. I think I know precisely how he felt.

Eight years later, as I poked around the Eisenhower White House in the guise of a consultant to the President-elect, I found myself impatient with the evident concern of thoughtful aides to tell me how they had done it, what they had learned. I was, after all, a busy man, with more memos to write! Granting that they might be better memos if I listened long and hard to what the "has-beens" had to say, nevertheless, my task was not an academic exercise, but rather something promised for tomorrow morning as the new sun rose, regardless of the old.

Self-importance separates incomers from outgoers, and this adds to sheer busyness as a source of hardened hearing. Eisenhower's science adviser, George Kistiakowski, a great chemist, a fine policy adviser, and a thoughtful courtier besides (literally, he had been a page in Petrograd at the Court of Nicholas II), became a friend when we were both at Harvard in the 1960s. He used to tease me about our first meeting at his office in the Old Executive Office Building, shortly before Kennedy took over. Kisty would pretend to be me, sit bolt upright in a chair, and say sharply, "Now, Professor Kistiakowski, tell me, if you can, why I should recommend that your Science Adviser's Office be continued. . . ."

As the memos in this book suggest, I was very much of that opinion and indeed put Kisty in the same class with Dulles, Hoover, and two others: someone who himself should be retained. So I would protest to him that I had not then been brash, merely direct, and was not demanding to be convinced, merely looking for ammunition. "No, Dick, whatever you say now, I think you were being brash," was always Kisty's rejoinder—with a chuckle.

The point, of course, is that if he thought so, I was. And if I was, I got less useful insights from him than I might otherwise have obtained. In later years, on friendly terms, I found him a mine of these.

The insights of thoughtful incumbents, still in office but already slated to leave, hence in a reflective mood, are an invaluable source of timely information on the way the government works, in a time span bound to be of relevance for their successors—whether or not the latter understand that at the start. What makes such lore invaluable is the sad fact that no institutional sources of memory exist as substitutes, save patchily, by happenstance, at higher executive levels of American government. Lore is almost all there is. Without it, available documentation tends to be ambiguous, misleading, or perverse.

Inadequacy of Institutional Memory. This is the third matter on which I wish to comment, and I do so mindful of a corollary, namely that such lore as is quite readily available is rather rarely consulted.

My colleague Ernest May and I once had occasion in the early 1980s to ask Dean Rusk, then in retirement, whether he had known about the Soviet army brigade in Cuba, the "discovery" of which had caused so great a flap during the Carter administration. Those troops had actually been there at the time of the missile crisis in 1962, but sixteen years later fresh photographic evidence surprised all Washington and caused the secretary of state, Cyrus Vance, to say that there would have to be a change in the status quo. Those words he had to eat when it eventually became clear that photographic evidence had been available all along, just not developed or consulted by officials who had reached their present jobs too late to hear or recall the old lore. Rusk told us that he remembered all about it: Kennedy had tried to get those troops removed, along with other things, had failed, and had decided not to press. Vance, then deputy secretary of defense, busy with different duties, had long since forgotten, if he ever knew. "I kept waiting for Vance to call me," Rusk informed us. "I'd have told him the whole story, but he never did call."[6]

That is not a transition story, not anyway in the "narrow" sense, but it is typical of what goes on inside a government where undersecretaries and assistant secretaries and White House chiefs of staff, and such all tend to come and go from their Washington jobs every second or third year, often even faster than rotating Pentagon brass or foreign service officers. It is a government, moreover, and has been at least since Nixon's time, where permanent officials of a civil service sort are ranked too low to serve reliably as accurate conveyors of what happens at top levels. By traditional British standards there scarcely is any institutional memory at all, save the lore in the heads of those who served before. Hurrah for the Rusks, although memory unused scarcely qualifies as "memory" at all.

During transition times, it is the Presidents-elect who are the greatest sufferers from lack of institutional memory. As I have noted, JFK was fascinated by the summary sketches I gave him on Franklin Roosevelt's staffing style. In a notable recent book, Matthew Dickinson has gone over that ground in far greater depth.[7] But as Dickinson himself points out, from Nixon's time through Clinton's, no incoming President could have known the ground, and even now they could discover it only by reading that book, an unlikely task in transition weeks, unthinkable in the two years or so before. This is so because, in the course of the 1960s, those who remembered FDR at first hand, and those who had been close to those who did, became so small a group, and so identified as Democrats, that no post-Goldwater Republican could respectably consult them. By the 1980s, they almost all had disappeared, leaving only Reagan to remember FDR as he had been—and Reagan's memories, evidently, were of the public Roosevelt, not the internal White House impresario.

In the United States, during the later years of the twentieth century, an entire chunk of administrative history, encompassing perhaps the most important Presidency of the century, certainly the longest-lived, dropped out of the consciousness of the entire political establishment. A Dickinson alone does not revive it.

The choice I offered Kennedy—and which he took, of course, because it appealed to his instincts, not my understanding—was never offered Nixon or his successors. Consciously or not, they built on, or amended, Nixon's first-term staffing pattern because, so far as they knew, it was the only one on offer.

Nixon himself began by adapting Eisenhower's pattern, which he personally had experienced. After a term of his own, Nixon innovated far-reaching changes for his second term, which might have led the way to a third alternative. But those he hastily withdrew, in four months' time, under Watergate pressure. Subsequent White House advisers scarcely noticed. Nor were they much aware that Roosevelt's ways had been generically different from the ones employed a generation later. There was almost nobody of their own age to tell them so and scarcely anyone of Roosevelt's left alive. Their journalistic counterparts were no wiser than they. Nor, for that matter, were most academics.

To the limited extent that contrasts with the 1940s figured in discussion during the transitions of the 1970s or after, they revolved around the question of a White House chief of staff. But that, by then, was a false issue. After Nixon—one might even say Johnson—the civilian aides within the White House proper, who claimed some share of responsibility for public policy, were just too numerous and varied to be managed by the President himself. The only one who tried it, Jimmy Carter, abandoned it in two years' time, with apologies to the nation.

"Management" by no means necessarily entails decision or direction of policy per se. What it does entail at a minimum, however, is direction of personnel: Who gets which offices, what pay grades, who gets to see which papers, who takes the lead on what assignments, who attends what meetings, who receives which visitors, who, at least among the lesser lights, gets hired, fired, and in to see the boss.[8]

Since Eisenhower's time those duties, at a minimum, have devolved on someone other than the President, or in Kennedy's case on three aides of especial seniority, in disciplined coordination with each other and with him. Since Nixon's time, with Carter's temporary exception, the someone has usually, not always, held the title Eisenhower first employed, "chief of staff," or has been the latter's deputy. Other, more avowedly substantive duties assigned to that same official have varied all over the lot, within administrations as well as between them. So has the character and quality of performance, by successive "chiefs," never more so than in Reagan's time and Clinton's. But the need for some such title and the use of it are taken as matters of course, nowadays, and have been for more than twenty years. Should FDR return to finish out his final term in the White House as currently staffed, I am sure he would have to designate a chief of staff (though probably with duties more minimal than otherwise).

The core difference between Roosevelt's staffing and Ike's, or later Kennedy's and Nixon's, was on an altogether different plane. Roosevelt saw the White House as the place for his personal business, the White House staff as his personal helpers in doing it, and the White House Office as a thing apart from the Executive Office of the President (which nominally included it). Setting aside the White House, as FDR in practice did, the EOP contained mainly the Budget Bureau (now OMB) and other more specialized entities concerned with the Presidency rather than with him personally. Those Executive Office units Roosevelt regarded as an aggregation of "institutional" assistants, almost all civil servants, distinct from his White House aides, who were almost all political appointees of his own selection.

Thus, FDR saw two presidential staffs in parallel, one tiny and personal, which he himself would manage, the other large and institutional, to be managed mainly by his appointee, the director of the budget, whose associate directors would all be civil servants. Roosevelt wished neither group to dominate the other and expected views on everything from both.

By contrast, Nixon, adapting from what he had seen under Eisenhower and expanding to suit himself, built up essentially one staff, with a greatly enlarged White House at the apex of a tall Executive Office pyramid. Virtually the whole of the quadrupled White House staff was appointive, but only the topmost few were Nixon intimates or his personal choices. At the same time, an increasing number of appointive posts were placed above the civil servants in Executive Office agencies. A heavily layered, appointive hierarchy of politically responsive aides, personally unknown to the President himself, came to stretch from just under the top reaches of the White House down to the upper-middle levels of the agencies, binding the whole together and erasing the distinction between personal and institutional.

No wonder that, over time, press usage has come to blur the difference between White House and Executive Office, tending to use the former term for both. But that distinction was of the essence of Roosevelt's style and is among the things that most appealed to JFK. I think no recent President has even known what it meant!

I do not make the point to argue for Rooseveltian staffs against other sorts, but rather to make plain, as forcefully as possible, the sheer dependence of incomers on what outgoers can tell them and, alas, at the same time, the variable quality of what the latter know. It all depends upon when they themselves came in. And yet their lore is most of what we have by way of institutional memory. Moral: Use it but do not trust it more than at most two presidential generations back, unless the oldsters can attest that they were personally present at an earlier creation!

Suspicion as a Bar to Knowledge

Transitions offer opportunities to extract a whole governmental generation's lore at once. But those who need it most and could best use it, the incomers, rarely think of such things. Busyness and self-importance bar the way and also, often, deep suspicion. That too is part of the conditions that apply to the eleven weeks. As such it too deserves a comment.

Three strands of suspicion come together in transition times. For one, the successful campaigners are suspicious of anyone who profits from their victory without having campaigned. On them and on their candidate, but no one else, a golden haze of brotherhood descended at the moment of election. It takes time to dissipate—for aides to small-state governors, more time perhaps than for others. Recall Hamilton Jordan's public complaints from Plains in 1976 (and what he did to Carter's hapless transition advisers).

For another thing, the outgoers suspect that their successors lack the competence to do their jobs. Recall the look on Eisenhower's face, encountering Kennedy in 1960!

And for a third thing—by far the most important—the incomers suspect that their inherited civil servants could be covert enemies, planted on them by their predecessors (whose party just lost the election). Recall John Foster Dulles in 1953, lecturing and hectoring his State Department employees. That year, the only parts of the federal government able to function fully from the start were the Budget Bureau and the Treasury—thus greatly advantaging them—whose heads had sensibly decided that they would trust their employees until shown otherwise. The rest of Ike's department heads took the opposite tack, like Dulles.

Mistrust of civil servants in 1953 was understandable, considering that many of their agencies had come into existence in the generation since Republicans had held the White House. Actually, Washington bureaucrats, like their fellow countrymen, voted for Ike in droves and keenly anticipated his arrival. But that was not instantly apparent to incomers who had been brought up hating Roosevelt.

By contrast, the permanent government was in relatively good repute when Ike gave way to Kennedy, only eight years later. The junior officers of World War II were merely taking over from their seniors, and the civil servants mostly had been on the scene in Truman's time. Suspicions of all three sorts have never been lower.

Even so, it is remarkable that in the run-up to the Bay of Pigs, JFK never once consulted his own secretary of the Treasury, Douglas Dillon, who until January 1961 had been Ike's undersecretary of state, chairing a committee meant to keep track of Dick Bissell. Dillon, in his new job, would not move beyond the confines of his bailiwick without an invitation. None came. Trails of suspicion can run deep, perhaps beneath consciousness.

Since Vietnam and Watergate, rising partisanship in Congress, press intrusiveness, negative TV, and lengthening campaigns have all contributed to making transitions more nearly resemble 1952 than 1960 in those regards. As Bell and I with Hauge, the outgoers tend perforce to stifle their suspicions, while disciplined staffs like Reagan's tend in time to stifle their campaigners. But allergic reactions by newcomers to the permanent government, including long-lived political appointees, are tripped off, nowadays, with every change of party. It is easy to see why. It also is unfortunate. For such reactions interfere with tapping the other side's lore.

Those are the conditions that obtain in the eleven weeks. After the extended nightmare of contemporary campaigning comes the truncated interval of preparation to take office, on a certain date in January, ready or not, while the whole country watches, interested in the novelty of the once-familiar candidate becoming President. Watching, too, are Congress, and the press corps, and a cabinet marked by strangers, and a permanent government whose measure has yet to be taken, and a staff that may not yet have jelled, all criss-crossed with mutual suspicions. And everyone is breathing down the neck of the new President.

What can he possibly make of it all?

A Final Comment

I conclude with a final comment. Imagine, as a good adviser should, arising after a long, itchy day and night to realization that the campaign years have ended and that you have been elected President of the United States, head of the only superpower in the world, as the cliché has it, and that in less than three months you will have been sworn in, responsible for everything from a congressional agenda to committing troops, from succoring flood victims to reassuring stockholders, from outwitting terrorists to launching fresh initiatives for peace in unlikely places.

Few human beings have to face and surmount the strain of switching suddenly from all-out campaigner in an atmosphere of sweaty effort, simple goals, to cooler tasks of governing amidst the endless ambiguities of complicated purposes and pressures. And in between there are, at once, the varied tasks—imperative yet scarcely understood from other people's recollections—of administration building in full view of a tetchy, hungry press corps. That strain, moreover, is not what it was in the last weeks of 1960, Kennedy's time for bipartisanship, or the last month of 1980, with Reagan's revolution on the verge, the hostages almost home, and the Democrats cowed by losing the Senate. The strain is not what it was; under current conditions it could well be worse.

Save for nuclear risks, currently in abeyance, all the conditions are harsher: The activists are louder on more fronts, the press is more insistent, Congress is less respectful, and the voters, seemingly, are soaked in cynicism tempered by prosperity. Yet Presidents-elect are under a necessity to keep their balance, and their temper, and their sense of humor—God willing that they have one—throughout the eleven weeks, so they can take them to the White House intact. For they will need them there, as will the country.

The imperative for their advisers, in transition time, is to acknowledge that, respect it, and facilitate it all they can. What do such advisers need most? In my estimation, two things: Empathy for their President-to-be. And for themselves, ego control.

Appendix

Additional Sources

Recent transitions have produced volumes of documents of various kinds. They include the specific memos from transition aides similar to those of Neustadt, countless reports from task forces and transition teams, independent reports from think tanks and professional organizations, manuals reflecting the experience of transition aides, and books that describe and analyze past transitions. The Presidential Transition Act of 1963 (as amended) has contributed to this volume of material by providing federal funds to the President-elect for the transition in and to the incumbent President for the transition out. The discussion here offers illustrations of those sources and what they may contribute.

Among the other most frequently cited memos is that by Clark Clifford, prepared for President-elect John F. Kennedy. The theme of Clifford's memo is revealed in the first sentence: "The turning over of government to a Democratic President elected today differs substantially from the transition to President-elect Eisenhower in 1952." In part, this observation was simply that of stating the governing preferences of a Democrat "not . . . suspicious or hostile to the Federal bureaucracy" as compared with those of a Republican. Associated, however, was Clifford's view, like that of Neustadt, that "the President-elect and his associates are well versed in major questions of policy and politics." Also like Neustadt, he advised Kennedy that Eisenhower's "board of directors" concept of the cabinet "should be junked." The remainder of the memo identifies White House staff positions to be filled, specifies liaison to other staff units, reviews major appointments, discusses relations with Congress (including major legislation), and advises control of the national party. Much of Clifford's treatment is straightforward—useful for the time it was written but bearing few lessons for the ages.

Stephen Hess, a senior fellow at the Brookings Institution, has published memos he prepared for President-elect Jimmy Carter in 1976–1977 and for Bill Brock, then chairman of the

Republican National Committee, in the spring of 1980. The memos appear in a book that, itself, is an important contribution to those involved in organizing a Presidency: *Organizing the Presidency,* 2d ed. (Washington, D.C.: Brookings Institution, 1988), appendixes A and B. The book provides a review and analysis of the Presidencies of Franklin Roosevelt through Ronald Reagan, as well as a more general treatment of the experience of organizing the White House and the selection and use of the cabinet.

Hess prepared his memos for Carter after being contacted by the President-elect. A former Nixon aide, Hess had solid contacts in the Ford White House. Then a Brookings scholar, Hess could serve as an independent liaison person for Carter to the Ford White House. After meeting with Richard Cheney, President Ford's chief of staff, Hess wrote a memo on staffing needs. Carter liked what he read and asked for more; eleven are published in Hess's book. Many of the standard topics are covered, though in the context of Carter's own decision in advance not to have a chief of staff. Among the most interesting and special memos is that dealing with "trappings." In it, Hess directs attention to the public imagery of the White House and the Presidency and recommends "tasteful symbolism," among other things. Hess also provides a thoughtful discussion of the role of the Vice President, one of the few available.

As with Neustadt's memo to Brountas for Dukakis, Hess's memo to Brock for Reagan is special for its sensible treatment of transition planning during the campaign. Hess wrestles with the problem of the cost of such planning, given the priority of campaign spending, and he outlines the types of organizational, political, and policy issues that accompany the prospect of winning in November. Thus, for example, he warned against transition planners' proposing policy or personnel before Election Day: "Even the hint that a transition group is 'writing policy' or 'picking people' will cause a maelstrom of dissension within the campaign organization."

There are, of course, innumerable memos written by aides that, while not publicly available, have circulated among subsequent transition teams and scholars of the process. In 1972, Theodore Sorensen prepared a comprehensive memo on standard transition issues at George McGovern's request. It was never delivered, given the outcome. He updated the memo four years later for use by Jimmy Carter. In early November 1973, Sorensen also prepared a unique document for Speaker of the House of Representatives Carl Albert. Impeachment proceedings were being called for on Capitol Hill following the so-called Saturday Night Massacre—the firing of Watergate special prosecutor Archibald Cox. Sorensen wrote Albert that he should be prepared should there be a vacancy in the White House before a new Vice President took office under the Twenty-Fifth Amendment (Spiro Agnew having resigned).[1]

Few transitions have been the subject of more advanced planning than that of Jimmy Carter in 1976. Early in the campaign, Carter selected a young Atlanta lawyer, Jack Watson, to prepare a plan during the campaign period. However effective and efficient, the planning was later compromised when campaign aides came to view Watson's group as threatening their winnings in the postelection period.[2]

Watson went at his task with energy and vigor, if limited coordination with the campaign staff. He faced a very different challenge from that of Neustadt. John Kennedy knew Washington and its politics; Jimmy Carter did not. The two sets of transition memos reflect that difference, in both style and substance. Stylistically, the Watson memos were lengthy (fifty-plus pages, double-spaced) and were offered the day after Carter's election. Neustadt's memos were terse by comparison, and the first one was presented to Kennedy in mid-September. Substantively, Watson was educating the President-elect, and himself, about the White House—its organization and relationships to other power centers. Neustadt could take much more for granted regarding the knowledge and political savvy of Kennedy and his staff.

Following the transition in 1980–1981, a bipartisan team produced a report for use in future transitions. The project was motivated by the lack of systematically collected basic information about transitions in for the winner and out for the incumbent. Thus, the report served as a manual in regard to the nitty-gritty issues. It provided detailed information on funding, organizational matters, administrative and housekeeping issues, staffing, transition teams, and even preparations for the first lady. Recommendations for managing future transitions are also provided. William Tucker of the Reagan representatives on the team coordinated the report; W. Harrison Wellford was the primary Carter representative. Entitled "Transition of the President and President-Elect," this report remains a most useful compendium of information for transition planners. In 1992 Wellford also prepared a work plan for staffing and organizing the White House and Executive Office of the President.

It is difficult to generalize about reports prepared by transition teams and task forces. The former are designed for the President-elect and his entourage to make contact with the government in place, notably the departments and agencies. The latter, task forces, are formed to prepare or refine specific policy proposals. The sheer volume of paper produced by those groups is staggering. Determining actual value for the transition is problematic, however, and many, probably most, are dumped not long after they are completed. In some cases, the actual reports may be less important than the learning that takes place among the group members. Or the groups may have been formed in part to provide interim jobs for campaign workers and liaison to important interest groups and law firms. Whatever the purpose, once cabinet and other major appointments have been made, the teams may be viewed as competitive with those charged with organizing the new administration. Note that Neustadt advised against task forces in his memo sent to Robert Reich "except on substantive issues of immediate concern where advice is really needed or big shots have to be conciliated." A Carter aide warned that such groups were "dangerous" because they "can easily veer out of control."[3] Transition teams, too, can foster expectations of appointments to the department or agency that is the subject of their review. The key for the positive use of such groups is clearly that of tight control by the transition directors.

Transitions in contemporary times have been accompanied by reports and recommendations by various Washington-based think tanks and professional organizations. Among the think tanks, the Brookings Institution has been the most active through the decades. As was noted in the introduction, Clark Clifford joined a Brookings panel on the transition in 1960. Also in that year, Brookings scholar Laurin Henry produced a detailed study of the four party-shift transitions, 1912–1952 (to Wilson, Harding, Roosevelt, and Eisenhower).[4] Other Brookings scholars have frequently been involved in transition teams, tasks forces, and study panels.

The National Academy of Public Administration has regularly offered advice on the appointing process, reorganization, and effective bureaucratic relations. The Carnegie Endowment for International Peace and other foreign policy and national security institutes have also been active in making recommendations for presidential transitions.[5] One of the most policy-oriented reports was produced in 1980 by the Heritage Foundation for the incoming Reagan administration. Entitled *Mandate for Leadership,* this 1,100-page book offered a detailed conservative agenda.[6] Similarly, the Progressive Policy Institute, a think tank associated with the Democratic Leadership Council, sought to influence the agenda of the new Clinton administration.

No President-elect in modern times lacks for outside advice as to how to organize and assign policy priorities. The challenge is, rather, to sort through the diverse offerings by well-meaning and sometimes self-serving analysts so as to judge which truly suit the purposes of the new administration. Put otherwise, a President-elect dependent on reports from think tanks or professional organizations is one unlikely to experience an effective transition.

The list of books on presidential transitions is not long, but several major works have been produced. Some are primarily historical, notably Laurin Henry's volume referred to above and the more recent treatment by Carl M. Bauer, *Presidential Transitions: Eisenhower through Reagan* (New York: Oxford University Press, 1986). As with Henry, Bauer provides a description and analysis of each of the transitions and concludes with observations about patterns and lessons. The Center for the Study of the Presidency has sponsored two compendiums on the transition: Bradley D. Nash, ed., *Organizing and Staffing the Presidency* (New York: Center for the Study of the Presidency, 1980), and James P. Pfiffner and R. Gordon Hoxie, *The Presidency in Transition* (New York: Center for the Study of the Presidency, 1989). As with all such collections, the entries vary enormously in their usefulness. Perhaps the most practical in the second volume are "Rumsfeld's Rules," the common-sense observations by Donald Rumsfeld, who served as chief of staff to President Ford. Among his recommendations for staff aides: "Don't play President—you're not."

Several books combine description and analysis of individual transitions along with a broader examination of general issues related to forming an administration. Stephen Hess's *Organizing the Presidency,* 2d ed. (Washington, D.C.: Brookings Institution, 1988) is a good example. Hess treats the organizational efforts of Roosevelt through Reagan in the context of recurring issues associated with the evolving Presidency. James P. Pfiffner has been a stalwart student of presidential transitions, one who has sought to promote understanding of the issues involved as an active participant in reports by the National Academy of Public Administration and through his frequent contact with transition aides. In *The Strategic Presidency: Hitting the Ground Running,* 2d ed. (Lawrence: University Press of Kansas, 1996), Pfiffner collates and integrates his experience and research, including interviews with all of those principally involved in recent transitions. The result is an informed and authoritative treatment of what is involved in creating a Presidency. My own book, *Passages to the Presidency: From Campaigning to Governing* (Washington, D.C.: Brookings Institution Press, 1998), stresses the immediate changes required for ending one intense activity—the presidential campaign—and beginning another—forming a Presidency. Attention is directed to the four recent party shifts—to Nixon (1968), Carter (1976), Reagan (1980), and Clinton (1992)—for the purpose of identifying the challenges facing future Presidents-elect. Among the special topics considered is the role of the press in the transition.

Several books focus on an individual President or a specific policy area. In the first category are memoirs and biographies that include descriptions of the transition. See, for example, Arthur M. Schlesinger, Jr., *A Thousand Days: John F. Kennedy in the White House* (Boston: Houghton Mifflin, 1965), and Edwin Meese III, *With Reagan: The Inside Story* (Washington, D.C.: Regnery Gateway, 1992). Bruce Adams and Kathryn Kavanagh-Baran provide a detailed study of the Carter transition in 1976 in *Promise and Performance: Carter Builds a New Administration* (Lexington, Mass.: Lexington Books, 1979). The book is a useful guide for what to avoid in forming a new Presidency. Aspects of the Kennedy transition are analyzed in Paul T. David, ed., *The Presidential Election and Transition, 1960–1961* (Washington, D.C.: Brookings Institution, 1961), and in David T. Stanley, *Changing Administrations* (Washington, D.C.: Brookings Institution, 1965). Foreign and national security policy is a major concern during a change of Presidents. It is the topic of a book by Frederick Mosher,

W. David Clinton, and Daniel G. Lang, *Presidential Transitions and Foreign Affairs* (Baton Rouge: Louisiana State University Press, 1987).

Finally, numerous books have been published on various activities related to the transition and early formation of a Presidency. Some representative works by category follow.

Appointments:

G. Calvin Mackenzie, *The Politics of Presidential Appointments* (New York: Free Press, 1981).

Staffing:

John Hart, *The Presidential Branch: From Washington to Clinton,* 2d ed. (Chatham, N.J.: Chatham House Publishers, 1995).

Samuel Kernell and Samuel L. Popkin, *Chief of Staff: Twenty-Five Years of Managing the Presidency* (Berkeley: University of California Press, 1986).

Bradley H. Patterson, Jr., *The White House Staff: Inside the West Wing and Beyond* (Washington, D.C.: Brookings Institution Press, 2000).

Management and Organization:

Peri E. Arnold, *Making the Managerial Presidency* (Princeton: Princeton University Press, 1986).

John P. Burke, *The Institutional Presidency* (Baltimore: Johns Hopkins University Press, 1992).

Colin Campbell, *Managing the Presidency: Carter, Reagan, and the Search for Executive Harmony* (Pittsburgh: University of Pittsburgh Press, 1986).

James P. Pfiffner, ed., *The Managerial Presidency,* 2d ed. (College Station: Texas A&M Press, 1999).

Charles E. Walcott and Karen M. Hult, *Governing the White House: From Hoover through LBJ* (Lawrence: University Press of Kansas, 1995).

Personnel and the Executive Branch:

Hugh Heclo, *A Government of Strangers: Executive Politics in Washington* (Washington, D.C.: Brookings Institution, 1977).
Thomas J. Weko, *The Politicizing Presidency: The White House Personnel Office, 1948–1994* (Lawrence: University Press of Kansas, 1995).

Agenda-Setting:

Jeff Fishel, *Presidents and Promises* (Washington, D.C.: Congressional Quarterly, 1985).
Paul C. Light, *The President's Agenda: Domestic Policy Choice from Kennedy to Reagan*, 2d ed. (Baltimore: Johns Hopkins University Press, 1991).

The Cabinet:

Jeffrey E. Cohen, *The Politics of the U.S. Cabinet: Representation in the Executive Branch, 1789–1984* (Pittsburgh: University of Pittsburgh Press, 1988).
Richard F. Fenno, Jr., *The President's Cabinet* (Cambridge: Harvard University Press, 1959).
Shirley Anne Warshaw, *Powersharing: White House–Cabinet Relations in the Modern Presidency* (Albany: State University Press of New York, 1996).

Press Relations:

Michael B. Grossman and Martha J. Kumar, *Portraying the President: The White House and the News Media* (Baltimore: Johns Hopkins University Press, 1981).
Stephen Hess, *The Washington Reporters* (Washington, D.C.: Brookings Institution, 1981), and *The Government/Press Connection* (Washington, D.C.: Brookings Institution, 1984).
Mark J. Rozell, *The Press and the Carter Presidency* (Boulder, Colo.: Westview Press, 1989); *The Press and the Ford Presidency* (Ann Arbor: University of Michigan Press, 1992); and *The Press and the Bush Presidency* (Westport, Conn.: Greenwood, 1996).

Notes

Notes

Part 1: The Editor's Introduction

1. Richard E. Neustadt, *Presidential Power and the Modern Presidents: The Politics of Leadership from Roosevelt to Reagan* (New York: Free Press, 1990), p. 248.

2. Remarks at the Woodrow Wilson International Center for Scholars, Smithsonian Institution, June 13, 1996, at a conference on "Presidential Power Revisited." In the 1990 edition of *Presidential Power*, Neustadt stated that "Kennedy's people leaped at governance." Neustadt, *Presidential Power and the Modern Presidents,* p. 241.

3. Quoted in Arthur M. Schlesinger, Jr., *A Thousand Days: John F. Kennedy in the White House* (Boston: Houghton Mifflin, 1965), p. 121.

4. Details are provided in Theodore C. Sorensen, *Kennedy* (New York: Harper & Row, 1965), p. 229. Sorensen states that the Brookings Institution "deserves a large share of the credit for history's smoothest transfer of power between opposing parties" (p. 229). There are several sources that discuss this period, including Carl M. Brauer, *Presidential Transitions: Eisenhower through Reagan* (New York: Oxford University Press, 1986), pp. 65–67; Clark Clifford (with Richard Holbrooke), *Counsel to the President: A Memoir* (New York: Random House, 1991), pp. 319–20.

5. Quoted in Schlesinger, *A Thousand Days,* p. 679. Schlesinger and Sorensen both recorded that Kennedy was somewhat annoyed by reports that he was essentially playing out Neustadt's *Presidential Power*, a conclusion Neustadt himself rejected in favor of the President's own understanding of political power and its uses. See Schlesinger, *A Thousand Days*, pp. 678–79, and Sorensen, *Kennedy*, p. 389.

6. Schlesinger, *A Thousand Days*, p. 124.

7. Sorensen, *Kennedy*, p. 230.

8. Clifford, *Counsel*, p. 325.

9. Two that were discussed—Health, Education, and Welfare, and the prospect of a Department of Urban Affairs—are not included here.

10. Memo to Sargent Shriver, "A White House Post for a Contact Man with Negro Groups," December 15, 1960.

11. For Neustadt's own account of the lessons from the Bay of Pigs, see Richard E. Neustadt and Ernest R. May, *Thinking in Time: The Uses of History for Decision Makers* (New York: Free Press, 1986), chap. 8.

12. Carter defeated Ford in 1976, but Ford was not elected, even as Vice President. He was the first to be appointed under the procedures of the Twenty-Fifth Amendment.

13. The most direct account by those involved is by Edwin Meese III, *With Reagan: The Inside Story* (Washington, D.C.: Regnery Gateway, 1992), chap. 5.

14. See Charles O. Jones, *Passages to the Presidency: From Campaigning to Governing* (Washington, D.C.: Brookings Institution Press, 1998), pp. 67–81, in which two types of transition planning during the campaign are identified: the integrated approach of the Nixon and Reagan efforts and the disassociated approach of Carter and Clinton.

15. James L. Sundquist, ed., *Beyond Gridlock? Prospects for Governance in the Clinton Years—and After* (Washington: Brookings Institution, 1993), p. 25.

16. This is a term used by Nelson W. Polsby to refer to the emergence of a White House political and policy apparatus separate from the executive branch. "Some Landmarks in Modern Presidential-Congressional Relations," in Anthony King, ed., *Both Ends of the Avenue: The Presidency, the Executive Branch, and Congress in the 1980s* (Washington: American Enterprise Institute, 1983), chap. 1. See also John Hart, *The Presidential Branch: From Washington to Clinton,* 2d ed. (Chatham, N.J.: Chatham House Publishers, 1995).

17. For details, see Jones, *Passages*, passim.

18. *United States Code Annotated*, Title 5, section 3110.

Part 4: The Author's Reflections

1. Television and radio interview, "After Two Years—A Conversation with the President," December 17, 1962, *Public Papers of the President, John F. Kennedy, 1962* (Washington, D.C.: Government Printing Office, 1963).

2. Charles O. Jones, *Passages to the Presidency: From Campaigning to Governing* (Washington, D.C.: Brookings Institution Press, 1998).

3. Arthur M. Schlesinger, Jr., *A Thousand Days: John F. Kennedy in the White House* (Boston: Houghton Mifflin, 1965), p. 123.

4. See *Brookings Study Group Report* (Washington, D.C.: Brookings Institution, 1960).

5. See my *Presidential Power and the Modern Presidents: The Politics of Leadership from Roosevelt to Reagan* (New York: Free Press, 1990), chaps. 11–13. See also Richard E. Neustadt and Ernest R. May, *Thinking in Time: The Uses of History for Decision Makers* (New York: Free Press, 1986), chaps. 4, 8.

6. Neustadt and May, *Thinking in Time*, pp. 93–96.

7. Matthew J. Dickinson, *Bitter Harvest: FDR, Presidential Power, and the Growth of the Presidential Branch* (New York: Cambridge University Press, 1997).

8. For enlargement of this theme, see "Does the White House Need a Strong Chief of Staff?" *Presidency Research* (Fall 1987); reprinted in James P. Pfiffner, ed., *The Managerial Presidency* (College Station: Texas A&M University Press, 1999), pp. 69–74.

Appendix: Additional Sources

1. The document is not public, but details are provided in a *Washington Post* story: "No. 1 House Democrat Was Ready and Willing to Succeed Nixon," November 28, 1982. Excerpts from Sorensen's memo are included.

2. For details, see Bruce Adams and Kathryn Kavanagh-Baran, *Promise and Performance: Carter Builds a New Administration* (Lexington, Mass.: Lexington Books, 1979).

3. Quoted in Charles O. Jones, *Passages to the Presidency: From Campaigning to Governing* (Washington, D.C.: Brookings Institution Press, 1998), p. 125.

4. *Presidential Transitions* (Washington, D.C.: Brookings Institution, 1960).

5. Two examples are Commission on Government Renewal, *Harnessing Process to Purpose* (Washington, D.C.: Carnegie Endowment for International Peace and Institute for International Economics, 1992), and Miller Center Commission on Presidential Transitions and Foreign Policy, *Transferring Responsibility: The Dangers of Transition* (Lanham, Md.: University Press of America, 1986).

6. Charles Heatherly, ed., *Mandate for Leadership* (Washington, D.C.: Heritage Foundation, 1981).

Index

Index

About the Author and the Editor

About the Author and the Editor

Richard E. Neustadt is Douglas Dillon Professor of Government Emeritus at the John F. Kennedy School of Government, Harvard University. For more than three decades an adviser to Presidents, their aides, and members of the cabinet, he is also the author of *Report to JFK: The Skybolt Crisis in Perspective* (Cornell University Press, 1999), *Presidential Power and the Modern Presidents: The Politics of Leadership from Roosevelt to Reagan* (Free Press, 1990), and, with Ernest R. May, *Thinking in Time: The Uses of History for Decision Makers* (Free Press, 1986).

Charles O. Jones is Hawkins Professor of Political Science Emeritus at the University of Wisconsin-Madison and a nonresident senior fellow at the Brookings Institution. He is a former president of the American Political Science Association and editor of the *American Political Science Review.* His recent books include *The Presidency in a Separated System* (Brookings Institution Press, 1994), *Passages to the Presidency: From Campaigning to Governing* (Brookings Institution Press, 1998), and *Clinton and Congress, 1993–1996: Risk, Restoration, and Reelection* (University of Oklahoma Press, 1999).

The American Enterprise Institute for Public Policy Research

Founded in 1943, AEI is a nonpartisan, nonprofit research and educational organization based in Washington, D. C. The Institute sponsors research, conducts seminars and conferences, and publishes books and periodicals.

AEI's research is carried out under three major programs: Economic Policy Studies; Foreign Policy and Defense Studies; and Social and Political Studies. The resident scholars and fellows listed in these pages are part of a network that also includes ninety adjunct scholars at leading universities throughout the United States and in several foreign countries.

The views expressed in AEI publications are those of the authors and do not necessarily reflect the views of the staff, advisory panels, officers, or trustees.